WALKING ON LA GOMERA AND EL HIERRO

About the Author

Paddy Dillon is a prolific walker and guidebook writer, with over 40 books to his name and contributions to many more. He also writes regularly for outdoor magazines and has appeared on radio and television.

Paddy has walked extensively around all the Canary Islands for this series of guides, along rugged cliff coasts, crossing deep and rocky *barrancos* and climbing all the highest mountains. He uses a palmtop computer to write as he walks. This makes his descriptions, written at the very point at which the reader uses them, highly accurate and easy to follow on the ground.

Paddy is an indefatigable long-distance walker who has walked all of Britain's National Trails and several major European trails. He lives on the fringes of the English Lake District and has led guided walking holidays and has walked throughout Europe, as well as in Nepal, Tibet, and the Rocky Mountains of Canada and the US. Paddy is a member of the Outdoor Writers and Photographers Guild.

Other Cicerone guides written by Paddy include:

WALKING ON LA GOMERA AND EL HIERRO

by

Paddy Dillon

2 POLICE SQUARE, MILNTHORPE, CUMBRIA LA7 7PY
www.cicerone.co.uk

© Paddy Dillon 2011

First edition 2011
ISBN: 978 1 85284 601 5

This book is the second in a new series of five guides to walking on the Canary Islands, replacing Paddy Dillon's previous Cicerone guides:

Walking in the Canary Islands, Vol 1: West
ISBN: 978 1 85284 365 6
Walking in the Canary Islands, Vol 2: East
ISBN: 978 1 85284 368 7

Printed by KHL Printing, Singapore

A catalogue record for this book is available from the British Library.
All photographs are by the author unless otherwise stated.

Advice to Readers

Readers are advised that, while every effort is made by our authors to ensure the accuracy of guidebooks as they go to print, changes can occur during the lifetime of an edition. Please check Updates on this book's page on the Cicerone website (www.cicerone.co.uk) before planning your trip. We would also advise that you check information about such things as transport, accommodation and shops locally. Even rights of way can be altered over time. We are always grateful for information about any discrepancies between a guidebook and the facts on the ground, sent by email to info@cicerone.co.uk or by post to Cicerone, 2 Police Square, Milnthorpe LA7 7PY, United Kingdom.

Front cover: The little village of Imada at the head of the Barranco de Guarimar on La Gomera (Walk 4)

CONTENTS

The path has been cut through a thick bed of ash, revealing a view of Valverde ahead

Map Key

———————	major roads
———————	walking route
••••••••••••••••••	alternative route or walk extension
▬ ▬ ▬ ▬ ▬ ▬	long-distance (GR) route
– – – – – – –	link
▪▪▪▪▪▪▪▪▪▪▪▪▪	dirt track
- - - - - - - -	seasonal river
———————	river
(sea shape)	sea
▥▥▥▥▥▥▥▥▥▥	tunnel
(town shape)	town
▲	peak
▪	habitation
●	mirador
•	fuente/spring
→	route direction
Ⓢ Ⓕ	start point/finish point
ⓈⒻ	start/finish point
Ⓐⓢ Ⓐⓕ	alternative start/alternative finish
ⒶⓈⒻ	alternative start/finish point
ⓌⒺ	walk extension

Contour Key

Map Scale

0   2   4km

	600–800m		1400–1600m
	400–600m		1200–1400m
	200–400m		1000–1200m
	0–200m		800–1000m
	sea level		

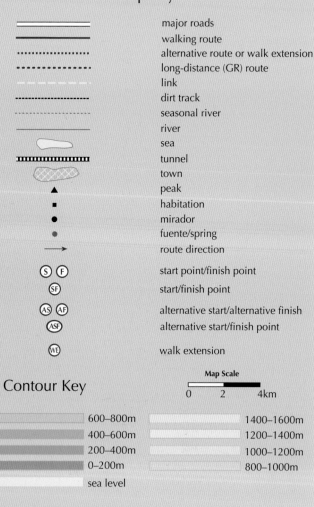

The Canary Islands

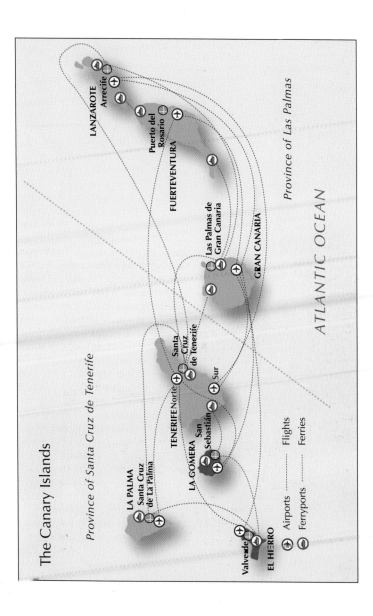

Province of Santa Cruz de Tenerife

Province of Las Palmas

ATLANTIC OCEAN

LANZAROTE
Arrecife

Puerto del
Rosario

FUERTEVENTURA

Las Palmas de
Gran Canaria

GRAN CANARIA

Santa
Cruz
de Tenerife

TENERIFE Norte

Sur

San
Sebastián

LA GOMERA

LA PALMA
Santa Cruz
de La Palma

Valverde

EL HIERRO

Airports ⊕   Flights ·········
Ferryports ◖   Ferries ·········

Deep in the Benchijigua valley near the little village of Pastrana, before a road-walk to Playa de Santiago (Walk 4)

INTRODUCTION

Starting the descent from La Mérica into Valle Gran Rey, using a broad and stony zigzag path (Walk 10)

The seven sub-tropical Canary Islands bask in sunny splendour off the Atlantic coast of north-west Africa. Millions of sun-starved north Europeans flock there for beach holidays, but increasingly visitors are discovering the amazing variety of landscapes throughout the archipelago. Conditions range from semi-deserts to perpetually moist *laurisilva* 'cloud forests', from rugged cliff coasts to high mountains, from fertile cultivation terraces to awesome rocky *barrancos* carved deep into multi-coloured layers of volcanic bedrock. Some areas are given the highest possible protection as national parks, but there are many more types of protected landscapes, rural parks, natural monuments and nature reserves.

More and more walkers are finding their feet, exploring the Canary Islands using centuries-old mule tracks, rugged cliff paths and forest trails. Paths pick their way between cultivation terraces, squeeze between houses and make their way to rugged coves and hidden beaches. Some paths run from village to village, following old mule tracks once used to transport goods, while other paths are based on pilgrim trails to and from remote churches and *ermitas*. Many have been cleared, repaired, signposted and waymarked in recent years, ready to be explored and enjoyed.

This guidebook explores the waymarked trail networks on the islands of La Gomera and El Hierro. Despite their small size, they boast routes of all types – from easy strolls to hands-on scrambling, from simple day-walks to long-distance trails. As these routes are fully signposted and waymarked, walkers can follow them with confidence and enjoy the islands to the full. Over 660km (410 miles) of trails are described in this guidebook.

LOCATION

The Canary Islands are more or less enclosed in a rectangular area from 13°30'W to 18°00'W and 27°30'N to 29°30'N. As a group, they stretch west to east over 450km (280 miles). Although administered by Spain, the mother country is 1100km (685 miles) away. The narrowest strait between the Canary Islands and Africa is a mere 110km (70 miles). The total land area is almost 7500km (2900 square miles), but the sea they occupy is ten times that size.

GEOLOGY

Most of the world's volcanic land-scapes are formed where huge continental or oceanic 'plates' collide with each other. When continental plates collide, the Earth's crust crumples upwards to form mountains, and when plates are torn apart, basaltic rock from deep within the Earth's mantle erupts to form mountains. The Canary Islands, however, are different, and have a complicated geological history.

The African landmass is the visible part of a continental plate that extends into the Atlantic Ocean, but the Canary Islands lie within the oceanic crust of the eastern Atlantic Ocean, close to the passive junction with the African continental plate. It is thought that the islands now lie directly above a hot-spot, or mantle plume, some 2500km (1550 miles) deep within the Earth. The mantle plume is fixed, but the oceanic and African plates are drifting very slowly eastwards. Every so often a split in the oceanic crust opens above the mantle plume, allowing molten rock to vent onto the ocean floor. As more and more material erupts, it piles higher and higher until it rises from the sea. Each of the Canary Islands was formed this way.

Lanzarote and Fuerteventura were the first Canary Islands to form, and were subsequently pulled eastwards. The next time a rift opened over the mantle plume the islands of Gran Canaria and Tenerife were formed, and these were in turn pulled eastwards. A further oceanic rift led to the formation of La Gomera, La Palma and El Hierro. Looking forward in geological time more islands will appear as other rifts are torn open in the future.

The forces at work deep within the Earth can scarcely be imagined. Every single piece of rock throughout the Canary Islands once existed in a molten state. Consider the energy needed to melt one small stone, and

El Teide on Tenerife is often seen above the clouds from La Gomera and El Hierro

multiply that to imagine the energy required to melt everything in the island chain, as well as the immense amount of rock beneath the sea that supports them all!

Over time huge amounts of volcanic material were piled high, but erosion has led to great instability. During recent geological time vast chunks of the islands have collapsed into the sea, creating features such as El Golfo on El Hierro, the Caldeira de Taburiente on La Palma, and the Orotava valley on Tenerife. With each catastrophic collapse, tidal waves devastated places around the Atlantic Ocean. Geologists predict that a similar collapse will take place in the future on the Cumbre Nueva on La Palma.

Plants and flowers

While the northern hemisphere was in the grip of an Ice Age, the Canary Islands were sluiced by rainstorms, with powerful rivers carving deep, steep-sided barrancos into unstable layers of ash and lava. As the landmasses emerged from the Ice Age the Canary Islands dried out and the vegetation had to adapt to survive. Some species are well adapted to semi-desert conditions, while on the highest parts of the islands, laurisilva cloud forests are able to trap moisture from the mists and keep themselves well watered. Laurisilva forests once spread all the way round Mediterranean and tropical regions, and one of the best remnants now

13

1 *Prickly pear fruit*

2 *The Canarian Tagasaste tree*

3 *Canarian lavender*

crowns La Gomera, where it is protected in a national park.

Canary pines flourish on high,
dry mountainsides, sometimes in
places where nothing else grows.
Almost every pine you see will have
a scorched trunk, but they regenerate surprisingly well after forest fires.
Beware of the long pine needles on
the ground, as they are slippery underfoot. Canary palms also flourish in dry
places, and in the past every part of
the tree had a use; today they pro-
vide delicious *miel de palma*, or palm
honey. Every so often dragon trees
occur, the last surviving descendants
of the ancient prehistoric forests. They
have been decimated in the wild but
prove popular in gardens.

Tagasaste trees are often found in
dense plantations, always in places
where livestock are grazed. They
grow with little water, yet have a high
nutritional content and are regularly
cut for animal fodder. In recent years
they have been exported to Australia.
Junipers are common; fruit and nut
trees have been established, including apples, oranges, lemons, bananas,
almonds, figs and vines. The intro-
duced prickly pears are abundant, not
so much for their fruit, but for raising
cochineal beetles, whose blood pro-
vides a vivid red dye.

Bushy scrub is rich and varied,
including sticky-leaved cistus and a
host of species that walkers should
learn to identify. These include bushy,

rubbery *tabaibal* and the tall *cardón*, or candelabra spurge. Both have milky latex sap, as does tangled *cornical*, with its distinctive horned seed pods, which creeps over the ground and drystone walls. *Aulaga* looks like a tangled mass of spines and is often found colonising old cultivation terraces in arid areas. Aromatic, pale green *incienso* is a bushy plant that, with *salado*, grows densely on the arid lower slopes of the islands. The fragrant Canarian lavender usually grows in arid, rocky, stony areas among other scrub species. Few of the plants have common English names, but all of them feature so often that they should be learned.

Flowers grow all year round, but visitors in spring and early summer will be amazed at the colour and wealth of flowering plants. Many are Canarian endemics, and even trying to compile a shortlist would be pointless. Anyone with a particular interest in flowers and other plants should carry a specific field guide, in English. Try *Native Flora of the Canary Islands* by Miguel Ángel Cabrera Pérez, Editorial Everest or *Wild Flowers of the Canary Islands* by David Bramwell and Zoë Bramwell, Editorial Rueda.

Animals

As befits remote islands created in relatively recent geological time, the main animal groups to colonise the land were winged creatures, insects and birds. The largest indigenous land mammals were bats. Large and small lizards also arrived, possibly clinging to driftwood. The laurisilva cloud

The giant lizards of El Hierro were rescued from the brink of extinction and are now being conserved

15

forest is home to the laurel pigeon, while the rock pigeon prefers cliffs. Buzzards and kestrels can be spotted hunting, and ospreys are making a slow come-back. Ravens and choughs are common in some places. There are several varieties of pipits, chaffinches, warblers and chiffchaffs. One of the smallest birds is the kinglet, a relative of the goldcrest. There are canaries, which have nothing to do with the name of the islands, and parakeets that add a flash of colour. The islands attract plenty of passage migrants, as well as escapees from aviaries. The coastal fringes are colonised by gulls, but it is best to take a boat trip to spot shearwaters or storm petrels, as they spend most of their time on open water. Boat trips are also the way to spot a variety of dolphins and whales.

Once the Guanche people arrived and colonised the islands over two thousand years ago, the forests suffered as much from clearance as from grazing by voracious sheep and goats. Following the Conquest in the 15th century, the Spaniards brought other domestic animals; of these the cats had a particularly devastating impact on the native wildlife, practically wiping out giant Canarian lizards, which have only recently been rescued from the edge of extinction. The largest of these lizards are on El Hierro, while the other islands have smaller species. Rabbits chew their way through the vegetation and appear regularly on Canarian menus.

16

NATIONAL PARKS

The Canary Islands contain a handful of national parks and many other protected areas. The Parque Nacional de Garajonay is in the middle of La Gomera, encompassing the highest parts which are densely covered in laurisilva forest. The whole island of El Hierro has been designated as a World Biosphere Reserve. Other protected areas on both islands include Parque Rural (Rural Park), Parque Natural (Natural Park), Paisaje Protegido (Protected Land), Reserva Natural Especial (Special Nature Reserve), Monumento Natural (Natural Monument), and so on. Prominent notices usually tell walkers when they are entering or leaving these areas. Very little territory lies outside one of these places! There are several visitor centres where more information can be studied, and where interesting literature is on sale.

THE FORTUNATE ISLES

Myths and legends speak of 'The Fortunate Isles', or 'Isles of the Blessed', lying somewhere in the Atlantic, enjoying a wonderful climate and bearing all manner of fruit. The rebel Roman general Sertorius planned to retire there, while Plutarch referred to them many times, though Pliny warned 'these islands, however, are greatly annoyed by the putrefying bodies of monsters, which are constantly thrown up by the sea'. Maybe these scribes knew of the Canary

Islands, or maybe they were drawing on older Phoenician or Carthaginian references. Some would even claim that the islands were the last remnants of Atlantis.

The Gaunches, often described as a 'stone-age' civilisation, settled on the Canary Islands well over 2000 years ago, and Cro-Magnon Man was there as early as 3000BC. No-one knows where the Guanches came from, but it seems likely that they arrived from North Africa in fleets of canoes. Although technologically primitive, their society was well-ordered, and they had a special regard for monumental rock-forms in the mountains.

The Guanches fiercely resisted the well-armed Spaniards during the15th century Conquest of the islands, but one by one each island fell. Tenerife capitulated last of all, with the mighty volcano of El Teide grumbling throughout. Many Guanches were slaughtered or enslaved, but some entered into treaties, converted to Christianity and inter-married. They lost their land and freedom, but their blood flows in the veins of native Canarios.

The Canary Islands were visited by Christopher Columbus on his voyage of discovery in 1492. Subsequently they were used as stepping stones to the Americas, and many Canarios emigrated. The islands were exposed and not always defended with military might; they were subject to pirate raids, endured disputes with the Portuguese, were attacked by the British and suffered wavering economic fortunes.

There was constant rivalry between Tenerife and Gran Canaria,

The original Guanche inhabitants of the Canary Islands fiercely resisted the Conquest

17

The Torre del Conde in San Sebastián on La Gomera Is one of the oldest remaining buildings

Canary Islands remained free of the worst strife of the Civil War, but also became something of a backwater. It was largely as a result of Franco's later policies that the Canary Islands were developed in the 1960s as a major destination for northern Europeans.

Since 1982 the islands have been an autonomous region and there have been calls for complete independence from Spain. The islanders regard themselves as 'Canarios' first and 'Spanish' second, though they are also fiercely loyal to their own particular islands, towns and villages.

GETTING THERE

There are no direct flights from the UK to La Gomera or El Hierro, but both islands are served from Tenerife. There are plenty of options for flying to Tenerife, scheduled or charter, from a range of British and European airports. The hardest part is checking all the 'deals' to find an airport, operator, schedules and prices that suit. Most international flights land at Tenerife Sur, but inter-island flights operate from Tenerife Norte. Transferring between airports can be expensive and time-consuming, and it may be easier to catch the next ferry.

Frequent, fast and cheap TITSA buses link Tenerife Sur with Los Cristianos, and the taxi fare is reasonable. If a night's accommodation is needed at Los Cristianos, there are large hotels that often have vacancies outside peak periods, such as the Sol

with the entire island group being governed from Las Palmas de Gran Canaria from 1808, before Santa Cruz de Tenerife became the capital in 1822. In 1927 the Canary Islands were divided into two provinces – Las Palmas and Santa Cruz de Tenerife.

In the early 20th century the military governor of the Canary Islands, General Franco, launched a military coup from Tenerife. This marked the onset of the infamous Civil War, leading to the creation of the Spanish Republic, and was followed by a long repressive dictatorship. The

18

Princesa Dácil. The bus stops, main hotels and ferryport are all within easy walking distance of each other. Two ferry companies operate to La Gomera and El Hierro: Lineas Fred Olsen and Naviera Armas.

WHEN TO GO

Most people visit the Canary Islands in summer, but it is usually too hot for walking. Winter weather is often good, but on the small islands of La Gomera and El Hierro there is frequent cloud cover on the highest parts, and occasional rain. Spring weather is sunny and clear; the vegetation is fresh and features an amazing wealth of flowers. Autumn weather is often good, but the vegetation often seems rather scorched after the summer.

ACCOMMODATION

Most visitors to the Canary Islands opt for a package deal, so they are tied to a single accommodation base in a faceless resort. This is far from ideal and a base in the 'wrong' place can make it difficult to get to and from walking routes. Package deals are seldom available on the islands of La Gomera and El Hierro; however, out of season, walkers would have no problem turning up unannounced on the doorsteps of hotels and pensións and securing accommodation. It is also possible to take short self-catering lets with ease. Simply obtain an up-to-date accommodation list from a tourist information office as soon as you reach one of the islands. Opportunities to camp are very limited. Wild camping is technically illegal, but it does take place.

The higher parts of La Gomera and El Hierro catch the clouds, especially in the winter months

HEALTH AND SAFETY

There are no nasty diseases on the Canary Islands, or, at least, nothing you couldn't contract at home. Water on La Gomera and El Hierro is either drawn from rainfall, or generated by the laurisilva cloud forests. It soaks into the ground, is filtered through thick beds of volcanic ash and emerges pure and clean, perfectly safe to drink. Bottled water is available if you prefer, but buy it cheaply from supermarkets rather than at considerable expense from bars. There are no snakes, no stinging insects worse than honey-bees, and there are always warning signs near hives. Don't annoy dogs and they won't annoy you. Dogs that are likely to bite are nearly always tethered, so keep away.

In case of a medical emergency, dial 112 for an ambulance. In case of a non-emergency, all islands have hospitals, health centres (*Centro de Salud*) and chemists (*Farmacia*). If treatment is required, EU citizens should present their European Health Insurance Card, which may help to offset some costs.

FOOD AND DRINK

Every town and most of the villages throughout the Canary Islands have bars. Most bars also double as cafés or restaurants, often serving tapas, which are often in glass cabinets, so you can point to the ones you want to eat. There are also shops, selling local and imported foodstuffs. Always make the effort to sample local fare, which is often interesting and very tasty. The

availability of refreshments is mentioned on every walking trail, but bear in mind that opening hours are variable. Some shops take a very long lunch break, and not all businesses are open every day of the week. Some shops are closed all weekend, or at least half of Saturday and all of Sunday.

LANGUAGE

Castilian Spanish is spoken throughout the Canary Islands, though in most resorts and large hotels there are English and German speakers. Those who travel to remote rural parts will need at least a few basic phrases of Spanish. Anyone with any proficiency in Spanish will quickly realise that the Canarios have their own accent and colloquialisms. For instance, the letter 's' often vanishes from the middle or end of words, to be replaced by a gentle 'h', or even a completely soundless gap. '*Los Cristianos*', for example, becomes '*Loh Cri-tiano*'. A bus is referred to as an *autobus* in Spain, but as a *guagua* throughout the Canary Islands. Some natives may seize the opportunity to practise their English with you, while others may be puzzled by your command of Spanish. No matter how bad you think you sound, you will not be the worst they've heard!

MONEY

The Euro is the currency of the Canary Islands. Large denomination Euro notes are difficult to use for small purchases, so avoid the €500 and €200 notes altogether, and avoid the €100 notes if you can. The rest are fine: €50, €20, €10 and €5. Coins come in €2 and €1. Small denomination coins come in values of 50c, 20c, 10c, 5c, 2c and 1c. Banks and ATMs are mentioned where they occur, if cash is needed. Many accommodation providers accept major credit and debit cards, as will large supermarkets, but small bars, shops and cafés deal only in cash.

COMMUNICATIONS

All the towns and some of the villages have post offices (*Correos*) and public telephones. Opening times for large post offices are usually 0830–1430 Monday to Friday, 0930–1300 Saturday, closed on Sunday. Small post offices have more limited opening times. Mobile phone coverage is usually good in towns and villages, but can be completely absent elsewhere, depending on the nature of the terrain. High mountains and deep barrancos block signals. In the past shepherds on La Gomera got round this problem by developing a whistling language, known as *Silbo*. Internet access is sometimes offered by hotels so, if relying on it, please check when making a booking.

WALKING IN LA GOMERA AND EL HIERRO

These are the two smallest Canary Islands, at the western end of the archipelago. La Gomera is heavily eroded, scored by dozens of steep-sided rocky barrancos. As a result, walks that lead in and out of them are often very

Pausing to watch a rainbow over the Hermigua valley on the way to the Cumbre (Walk 24)

rugged, but that shouldn't suggest that the walking is going to be too difficult for 'ordinary' walkers. In fact, almost all the routes in this guidebook follow waymarked trails, made up of narrow paths and broad tracks that often zigzag to ease the gradient.

Access to the coast is often limited to the mouths of the barrancos, as there are sheer cliffs elsewhere. By contrast, the highest parts of the island are much gentler and are covered in extensive laurisilva forest, encircled by pines. On El Hierro the laurisilva forest is less extensive and there are more pines. Barrancos are not as deep and rugged, and instead there are extensive slopes of volcanic ash and dozens of well-defined volcanic cones.

On both islands, traditional paths have been cleared, repaired, signposted and waymarked to create splendid trail networks.

WHAT TO TAKE

If planning to use one or two bases to explore, then a simple day pack is all you need, containing items you would normally take for a day walk. Waterproofs can be lightweight and might not even be used. Footwear is a personal preference, but wear what you would normally wear for steep, rocky, stony slopes, remembering that hot feet are more likely to be a problem than wet feet. Lightweight, light-coloured clothing is best in bright sunshine, along with a sun hat and frequent applications of sunscreen.

If planning to backpack around the islands, bear in mind that wild camping is technically illegal, though surprisingly popular. Lightweight kit should be carried, as a heavy pack is a cruel burden on steep slopes in hot weather. **Note** Water can be difficult to find, so try and anticipate your needs and carry enough to last until you reach a village, houses or bar where you can obtain a refill. (All such places are indicated in the text.)

WAYMARKING AND ACCESS

Both La Gomera and El Hierro share the same system for signposting and waymarking routes, using standard European codes. Both islands have a network of short PR (*pequeño recorrido*) routes, which are marked with yellow and white paint flashes, and numbered to keep them separate. Signposts will read PR LG on La Gomera, and PR EH on El Hierro, with a number following the letters.

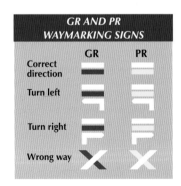

GR AND PR WAYMARKING SIGNS

	GR	PR
Correct direction		
Turn left		
Turn right		
Wrong way		

These codes are quoted in the route descriptions so that walkers will always be able to check they are going the right way. Both islands also have GR (*gran recorrido*) routes; these are intended as long-distance walks, but can also serve as simple one-day linear walks.

Apart from signposts, routes are marked by occasional paint marks: parallel yellow and white stripes for the PR routes, and red and white stripes for the GR routes. These confirm that walkers are still on course, and usually appear at junctions. Left and right turns are indicated with right-angled flashes, but if the paint marks form an 'X', this indicates that a wrong turn has been made.

1 *La Gomera and El Hierro boast splendid networks of signposted and waymarked short and long trails*

2 *A signpost at a junction of tracks and paths marks an important link with the village of Sabinosa (Walk 39)*

3 *The long-distance GR 131 at starts at Orchilla on El Hierro among twisted lava and volcanic ash*

MAPS

The Instituto Geográfico Nacional (IGN), www.cnig.es, publishes maps of the Canary Islands at scales of 1:50,000 and 1:25,000. These are part of the Mapa Topográfico Nacional (MTN) series. To avoid disappointment, please check the style and quality of these maps before making a purchase, since they generally do not show the details that walkers require.

For La Gomera the best map of the island and its network of sign-posted trails is the one seen mounted on map-boards around the island. It is rather annoying that all this fine detail has been mapped, yet the map itself is not available for purchase. Hopefully, it will be available one day, and in the meantime walkers can refer to the information in this guidebook, and supplement the guide with another map. The 1:30,000 Kompass map of La Gomera is good, and this is available in Britain with an Automobile Association cover, as the AA Island Series 8 – La Gomera.

On El Hierro the tourist informa-tion offices provide a free map of the trail network, which can be used with a topographical map. The 1:30,000 Kompass map of El Hierro is good, and this is available in Britain with an Automobile Association cover, as the AA Island Series 5 – El Hierro.

Maps can be ordered in advance from British suppliers such as: Stanfords (12–14 Long Acre, London, WC2E 9BR, tel. 020 7836 1321, www. stanfords.co.uk), The Map Shop (15 High Street, Upton-upon-Severn, WR8 0HJ, tel. 01684 593146, www.themap shop.co.uk) or Cordee (11 Jacknell Road, Dodwell Bridge Industrial Estate, Hinckley, LE10 3BS, tel. 01455 611185, www.cordee.co.uk).

The route maps in this guide are all at 1:200,000 scale with north to the top.

EMERGENCIES

The pan-European emergency tel-ephone number 112 is used to call for assistance throughout the Canary Islands, linking with the police, fire or ambulance service, for a response on land or at sea. The Guardia Civil telephone number is 062, and it is likely that they would be involved in a response involving mountain rescue, as they generally patrol rural areas.

USING THIS GUIDE

Two islands are covered in this guide-book – La Gomera and El Hierro – each with their own introduction. The walks are spread roughly clock-wise around the islands, and where they lie side-by-side, links between routes are often possible. On both islands, after several day walks have been described, there are also long-distance walks. Both islands feature coast-to-coast trails, while La Gomera also features a circular trail taking up to a week to complete. Any day-long stretch can naturally also be followed as a walk in its own right, using bus services to join and leave it.

On arrival at either island, visit the tourist information office as soon as possible. Ask for an accommoda-tion list, an up-to-date bus timetable and as much information about walk-ing opportunities as they can pro-vide. Remember to pick up leaflets about local attractions for full contact details, opening times and admission charges.

LA GOMERA

The resistant volcanic stump of Roque de Agando towers over the Benchijigua valley (Walk 4)

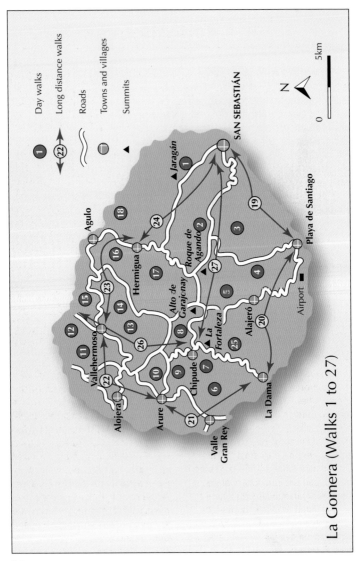

Key

- Day walks
- Long distance walks
- Roads
- Towns and villages
- Summits

La Gomera (Walks 1 to 27)

INTRODUCTION

Looking down on the Ermita de San Juan, with El Teide on Tenerife far beyond (Walk 17)

La Gomera is a small circular island that supports a wealth of walking opportunities. It takes time to explore and this guidebook alone contains a month's walking. The main settlements are located near the sea, but the roads linking them have to cross the high, forested parts of the island. There is no coastal road because dozens of steep-sided, rocky barrancos would have to be negotiated. Walkers, on the other hand, can enjoy trekking in and out of these canyon-like barrancos, crossing the high ridges between.

Over 400km (250 miles) of walking on La Gomera are described in this book, divided into 27 days. There are 18 one-day walks, signposted as PR (*pequeño recorrido*) routes, and a further nine days signposted as GR (*gran recorrido*) routes, which can be linked together as long-distance walks. Very few of these routes stand in isolation, and most of them link with one, two or more adjacent routes, so there are options to alter and adapt them, and some routes feature significant variants and extensions.

Readers will notice that the GR131 is described across La Gomera and El Hierro, offering coast-to-coast routes. In fact, there is much more to this trail, which is planned to stretch across all seven Canary Islands. Furthermore, the trail is part of the pan-European E7 route. On a more local scale, the GR132 offers a circular long-distance walk around La Gomera, taking anything up to a week to complete.

GETTING THERE

By Air

Flights from Tenerife Norte to La Gomera are operated by Binter Canarias, tel. 902-391392, www.binter canarias.com. There are no flights from Tenerife Sur. Buses meet incoming flights offering links with Playa de Santiago, San Sebastián and Valle Gran Rey. Taxis are also available at the airport.

By Ferry

Two ferry companies operate between Los Cristianos on Tenerife, and San Sebastián on La Gomera. Lineas Fred Olsen, tel. 902-100107, www. fredolsen.es, is quick and expensive. Naviera Armas, tel. 902-456500, www.naviera-armas.com, is slower and cheaper. Ferries berth almost in the centre of San Sebastián, within walking distance of all facilities and the bus station. Both ferry companies also sail between La Gomera and El Hierro.

GETTING AROUND

By Bus

La Gomera has a good network of bus services operated by Servicio Regular Gomera, tel. 922-141101. There is no website and information on the internet is unreliable. Obtain an up-to-date timetable for the whole island as soon as possible, from bus stations or tourist information offices. Tickets are for single journeys and fares are paid on boarding the bus. Buses are referred to as 'guaguas', although bus stops, or paradas, may be marked as 'bus'. All the towns and most villages have buses. Most visitors do not realise that the little mountain village of Chipude has the best level of services and destinations. The capital, San Sebastián, on the other hand, does not have particularly good links with some parts of the island.

By Taxi

Long taxi rides are expensive, but short journeys are worth considering. Taxi ranks are located at San Sebastián, tel. 922-870524, Playa de Santiago/Alajeró, tel. 922-895022, Valle Gran Rey, tel. 922-805058, Vallehermoso, tel. 922-800279, Agulo, tel. 922-801074 and Hermigua, tel. 922-880047. Fares are fixed by the municipalities and can be inspected on demand, though negotiation might be possible.

Planning your Transport

To make the most of walking opportunities, and limit long and awkward travelling, it is best to choose two or three accommodation bases with good bus connections. Using a car is not always a good idea, especially when following linear routes.

Linear routes described in this book always start at the 'awkward' end, usually high in the mountains, to which you would need to take a taxi, and finish where you can catch a bus. The introduction to each walk has a note about the availability of public transport. If no bus is mentioned serving the start or finish, then the use of a taxi will be required.

The route maps in this guide are all at 1:200,000 scale with north to the top.

ACCOMMODATION

Accommodation is abundant around La Gomera, and it is best to obtain an up-to-date list from a tourist information office if walking from place to place. At the top end of the scale are the Parador at San Sebastián and the Hotel Jardin Tecina at Playa de Santiago. There are other hotels around the island, as well as simple pensións and self-catering apartments, with prices to suit all pockets. The Hotel Sonia in Chipude is an excellent base, not only because of the immediate variety of walks but also because it has good bus links.

FOOD AND DRINK

La Gomera is self-sufficient in terms of fruit, vegetables and fish. While some restaurants are cosmopolitan, others offer good local fare. Specialities include goat cheese. Most is eaten just as it is. Some goat cheese, but only a little, is used to make an oily sauce called almogrote. Watercress soup (sopa de berros) sounds bland but is very tasty. Wrinkly potatoes (papas arrugadas) cooked in salt are surprisingly refreshing in hot weather, served with hot mojo roja sauce and gentler mojo verde.

The most popular fish dishes are based on vieja. If any dishes such as soups or stews need thickening, then reach for the roasted flour gofio, which also serves as a breakfast cereal. Many desserts are enhanced with miel de palma, or palm honey, a dark syrup from Canarian palm trees. There are also Gomeran wines available. Never pass an opportunity to indulge in local fare!

TOURIST INFORMATION OFFICES

San Sebastián, tel. 922-141512
Playa de Santiago, tel. 922-895650
Valle Gran Rey, tel. 922-805458

WALK 1

San Sebastián and Jaragán

Distance	18km (11 miles)
Start/Finish	Plaza de la Constitución, San Sebastián
Total Ascent/Descent	700m (2295ft)
Time	5hrs
Terrain	Roads, tracks and rugged paths on the ascent. A steep descent and a long road walk to finish.
Refreshment	Plenty of choice in San Sebastián. Bars at Lomo Fragoso and El Langrero.
Transport	Buses converge on San Sebastián from all parts of La Gomera.

After climbing from the centre of San Sebastián to its highest suburbs, tracks give way to rugged mountain paths across the face of Jaragán. A ridge walk is followed by a steep and rugged descent through scrub into a valley. A simple road walk returns to San Sebastián.

Route uses PR LG 1 and GR 132.

Start in the centre of **San Sebastián** on a corner of the Plaza de la Constitución beside the Bar Restaurante La Hila. Walk up the narrow Camino de La Hila and turn right. The stone-paved street climbs, ending with steps to the **Mirador de La Hila**. Enjoy the views and continue up the road, keeping right at a junction signposted for La Lomada. At the next road bend, climb steps up Camino de Puntallana. Watch for a right turn up more steps and climb to a road at a higher level. Turn left and keep left at a junction to pass the little Pescadería San Cristóbal. The road climbs and leaves the top end of town.

Reach a roundabout and follow a narrow road uphill. Turn right as signposted for Jaragán, following a path through tabaibal, verode and aulaga vegetation. Cross a water pipe and head gently up to a narrow road. Turn

right then quickly left to walk up beside a goat enclosure to reach the road again at a signpost. Walk up an easy, stony path past old terraces on **Lomo de Las Nieves**. The path levels out with views across the valley to Los Roques, with Jaragán ahead.

The harbour at San Sebastián, with the rugged mountain of Jaragán rising far beyond

Follow the path onwards and go down a rocky ramp above palms. Cross a gap and climb, exploiting a soft red layer. Climb onto a ridge and pass lots of cardón and tabaibal scrub. Rocks have been shifted to make the path, but watch carefully as it rises across a slope of prickly pears. A pointed peak rises ahead, so keep right and pick up a path contouring along a soft, creamy layer of rock. Later, zigzag up towards palms then head downhill. The path contours round a hollow in the mountainside around 500m (1640ft). A reddish, stony zigzag path cuts through old terraces, becoming vague as it crosses the shoulder of **Jaragán** around 625m (2050ft).

Swing right along another soft, creamy layer on the rocky slope, slicing across the face of Jaragán, sometimes cut so deeply that the rock overhangs. Dogs may be heard barking up the cliff, at a little goat farm. Keep

31

The dirt road can be followed right for Hermigua. It is easy, but very long and convoluted.

following the terrace path onwards, wary of rock-fall. When the far end of the ridge is reached, scooped-out steps lead downhill and a sign announces the Parque Natural Majona. Zigzag down to a bend on a dirt road at 599m (1965ft), and make a decision. ◄

The dirt road can be followed left, winding easily down to the main road, but the PR LG 1 is signposted up a rocky path instead. It starts awkwardly but becomes easier, climbing a broad ridge between forest and scrub. Climb only

until a path drifts left, linking with a narrow, stone-paved path zigzagging down a steep slope of dense scrub. Signposts beside the main road at the bottom point through a barrier for Las Casetas and Lomo Fragoso.

Follow a short stretch of dirt road, but turn left down a narrow zigzag path on another steep and scrubby slope. When a house is reached, turn left

The path across the face of Jaragán is very narrow and at times runs beneath an overhang

down a red-tiled path, cross a streambed, go down steps and pass some banana plants. Turn left to cross a bridge over a river then turn right to reach a road beside the Bar El Atajo at **Lomo Fragoso**. The return to San Sebastián is a simple road walk. ▶

See end of Walk 24 for details.

La Hila

SAN SEBASTIÁN

WALK 2
Los Roques and La Laja

Distance	8.5km (5¼ miles)
Start/Finish	Degollada de Peraza
Total Ascent/Descent	700m (2295ft)
Time	4hrs
Terrain	Good paths and tracks, sometimes on very steep slopes. Fine valley and mountain views, though some parts are forested.
Refreshment	Bar at Degollada de Peraza.
Transport	Buses reach Degollada de Peraza from San Sebastián, Playa de Santiago and Valle Gran Rey.

Motorists can start this walk at La Laja, climb to Los Roques, head for Degollada de Peraza and finish by descending to La Laja. Non-motorists can reach Degollada de Peraza by bus. The route follows fine stone-paved paths and includes remarkable scenery at Los Roques.

Route uses PR LG 17 and GR 131. If starting from La Laja, find an electricity transformer tower on a road bend. Go down steps and turn right. Cross a concrete bridge over a stream. Zigzag up past houses and turn right as signposted for Los Roques.

Buses stop at just over 900m (2950ft) at **Degollada de Peraza**, where there is a map-board and nearby bar restaurant. Follow the PR LG 17 downhill for La Laja. The steep, winding, stone-paved path offers splendid views across the valley. Aloes, cistus and asphodel grow beside the path, with pines and tabaibal further down, and palms later.

Pass a ruined *caseta* and prickly pears. After turning round a side valley there is a good view of La Laja, with pines rising to the domes of Los Roques. Stone-paved zigzags drop into a valley. Climb up the other side, cross a slight gap and pass an almond tree. The path zigzags down past palms and reaches the first few houses in **La Laja**. Turn left as signposted for Los Roques. ◀

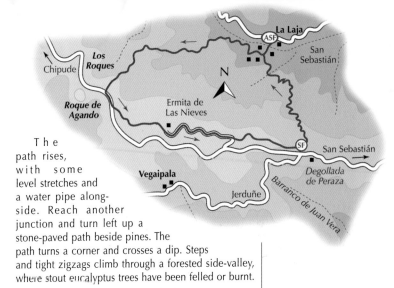

The path rises, with some level stretches and a water pipe alongside. Reach another junction and turn left up a stone-paved path beside pines. The path turns a corner and crosses a dip. Steps and tight zigzags climb through a forested side-valley, where stout eucalyptus trees have been felled or burnt.

Sunshine on the little village of La Laja, with misty mountains rising all around

35

A ruined caseta sits on a gap high above la Laja, with the rocky domes of Los Roques beyond

Leave the valley and start a climbing traverse across a slope of pines, crossing a couple more side-valleys on footbridges. There is a slight drop into another side-valley to cross another footbridge then the path climbs through the forested valley. A gap and a crumbling caseta are reached, with the mighty domes of Los Roques beyond.

Turn left up a path and pass a 'limite del parque' notice. Heather trees appear as the path climbs the forested crest. The Roque de Agando comes into view and the broad path ends with flights of stone steps climbing to a main road. For a closer view of **Roque de Agando** turn right; otherwise turn left to return to Degollada de Peraza. The PR LG 17 runs in tandem with the GR 131 beside the main road. ◂

See the middle of Walk 27 for the route back to the start.

WALK 3

Risco de la Fortaleza

Distance	15km (9½ miles)
Start/Finish	Degollada de Peraza
Total Ascent/Descent	600m (1970ft)
Time	6hrs
Terrain	Rugged paths across steep slopes and cliff faces.
Refreshment	Bar at Degollada de Peraza.
Transport	Buses reach Degollada de Peraza from San Sebastián, Playa de Santiago and Valle Gran Rey.

Risco de la Fortaleza is completely surrounded by cliffs on a rocky ridge high above San Sebastián and Playa de Santiago. A rugged path approaches it, and an interesting circuit takes in ruined farmsteads on exhausted, arid terraces at Morales and Casas de Contreras.

Buses stop at just over 900m (2950ft) on **Degollada de Peraza**, where there is a map-board and a nearby bar restaurant. Follow the road signposted down to Playa de

Route uses PR LG 18, PR LG 18.1 and GR 132.

Little casetas are passed soon after the start of the walk alongside Risco de la Fortaleza

Santiago, to find a signpost on the left at a rock cutting near **Jerduñe**, indicating the PR LG 18. The path is on a crest, but drops gently to the right across a steep and rocky slope, passing palms and aloes to reach ruined casetas overlooking the **Barranco de los Castradores**.

Go down rugged and easy stretches of path, passing palms, aloes, prickly pears, cistus, tabaibal and tagasaste. The path is mostly downhill, but there are a couple of short, steep, stone-paved ascents on the slopes of **Risco de la Fortaleza**. Eventually, the path turns gradually left and levels out among palms and aloes. Rise past terraces to reach a gentle gap at **Llano de la Cruz**, around 720m (2360ft).

There is a path junction, and the plan is to turn left along the PR LG 18.1, return to this point later on the PR LG 18 and then retrace the route back to Degollada de Peraza. First, turn left as signposted for Morales. The path climbs gently before descending, Note a solitary ruin, but keep an eye on yellow/white flashes as the path crosses old terraces covered in tabaibal. Drift towards the edge of the Barranco del Cabrito, then away from it, then back towards it.

Walk down towards a ruin, but watch for a sudden right turn away from the barranco. The path leads down to another ruin, then afterwards turns left at a junction to pass yet another ruin. Level out and reach a signpost at the ruined village of **Morales**, around 520m (1705ft). ◄

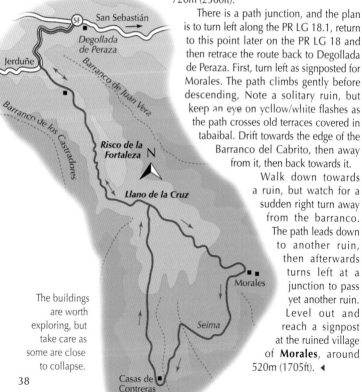

The buildings are worth exploring, but take care as some are close to collapse.

38

Turn right, as signposted for the GR 132 for Casas de Contreras, down a rocky path to cross a barranco, then up across a slight gap. Go down to cross another barranco then up across a terraced slope. The path drifts down to a rock wall, which is climbed using a breach; then a gentle descent crosses a terraced slope. A rugged path drops into a barranco and climbs up the other side past a ruin. Watch carefully at a corner, turning right to drop into a deeper barranco. Climb the other side to a ruined mansion at **Casas de Contreras**, at 400m (1310ft).

Turn right at the crumbling ruins of **Casas de Contreras** as signposted uphill for the PR LG 18 for Degollada de Peraza. Climb past the house and the prickly pears behind it. Go up a rocky, boulder-paved path that rises along a low, rocky ridge between terraces covered in tabaibal. Keep climbing to pass three ruins and the path finally levels out at **Llano de la Cruz**, returning to the path junction reached earlier in the walk. Turn left downhill, as signposted for the PR LG 18, and simply retrace the earlier steps of the day to return to **Degollada de Peraza**.

The substantial ruined house among arid old terraces at Casas de Contreras

39

WALK 4

Los Roques and Benchijigua

Distance	13km (8 miles)
Start	Roque de Agando
Finish	Playa de Santiago
Total Ascent	75m (245ft)
Total Descent	1200m (3935ft)
Time	5hrs
Terrain	A steep initial forested descent, then more gently graded valley paths, ending with a long road walk to the coast, or an optional climb.
Refreshment	Plenty of choice in Playa de Santiago.
Transport	Buses serve Los Roques from San Sebastián and Valle Gran Rey. Buses from Playa de Santiago serve San Sebastián and Valle Gran Rey.

Los Roques represent the resistant innards of ancient volcanoes, forming a remarkable huddle of rocky domes. Walking southwards leads through the scenic and often dramatic Benchijigua valley. The route ends with an easy road walk to Playa de Santiago, with an option to climb and finish at Imada.

Route uses PR LG 16, with an option to follow PR LG 16.1.

There are also aloes, tagasaste, almonds, prickly pears, cistus and all kinds of low-lying plants.

Start at the foot of the **Roque de Agando**, over 1100m (3610ft), where it is worth climbing up and down the steps to take in a series of remarkable roadside viewpoints. The path leaving the road is signposted for Benchijigua and immediately enters the Reserva Natural Integral Benchijigua. Laurisilva quickly gives way to pines as the stone-paved path winds downhill. ◄ Cross a concrete water channel and continue down a narrow path.

Cross a stream and head gently up an easier path, with views back to Roque de Agando. A level path

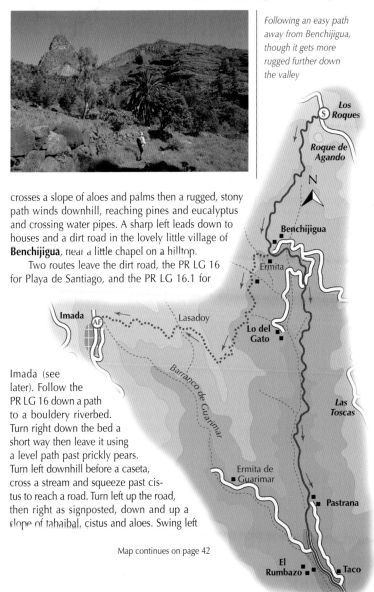

Following an easy path away from Benchijigua, though it gets more rugged further down the valley

crosses a slope of aloes and palms then a rugged, stony path winds downhill, reaching pines and eucalyptus and crossing water pipes. A sharp left leads down to houses and a dirt road in the lovely little village of **Benchijigua**, near a little chapel on a hilltop.

Two routes leave the dirt road, the PR LG 16 for Playa de Santiago, and the PR LG 16.1 for Imada (see later). Follow the PR LG 16 down a path to a bouldery riverbed. Turn right down the bed a short way then leave it using a level path past prickly pears. Turn left downhill before a caseta, cross a stream and squeeze past cistus to reach a road. Turn left up the road, then right as signposted, down and up a slope of tabaibal, cistus and aloes. Swing left

Map continues on page 42

round a corner on an ash slope. Wind down to cross a water channel and a streambed. The path runs part way down the valley, passing palms, then follows a terrace with a view across to the little village of **Lo del Gato**.

Avoid a sharp right turn to the village, keeping straight ahead along stone-buttressed paths above the river. Wind down past two circular reservoirs and follow pipes a short way as waymarked. Cross the rocky riverbed and walk down it to reach a building. Continue down the riverbed and cross it to climb up a stone-paved zigzag path. Follow a terrace path past houses and gardens, then a concrete path with steps to a road at **Pastrana**.

Follow the road a little then turn right to zigzag down steps and a rugged path to reach a road in the valley bottom. Turn left to follow it past palms, canes and cardón. Pass two bridges, the second one having a map-board and signpost at **El Rumbazo**. The PR LG 15 joins the PR LG 16 and both routes continue to Playa de Santiago. ◀

To climb to Targa and Alajeró, see Walk 5.

Follow the road up to a junction near **Taco**, keeping straight ahead downhill. The scenery becomes cluttered with pylons, telegraph poles, water pipes and a sprawling stone-works. Reach a junction with a main road near a tunnel, and walk straight ahead along a road marked 'no entry' to pass bananas. A couple of shops and a bus shelter lie at the end of the road at **Laguna de Santiago**. Turn right along the road, Paseo de La Laguna, which leads through banana plantations onto the Promenade Avenida Maritima through Playa de Santiago. The resort offers a full range of services and facilities. Apartments, pensión, banks with ATMs, post office, shops, bars, restaurants, buses and taxis. Tourist information office, tel. 922-895650.

El Rumbazo

Taco

Barranco de Santiago

Tunnel

Laguna de Santiago

Ⓕ Playa de Santiago

The little village of Imada is tucked away at the head of the rugged Barranco de Guarimar

Optional Ascent to Imada

This is shorter than the main route, but climbs over 300m (985ft). Leave **Benchijigua** via the PR LG 16.1, along a track that usually has a chain across. Follow it gently downhill and as it levels out. Keep right at a junction then bend left across a streambed in a small valley full of palms. Watch for a narrow, well-trodden path off to the right, opposite an old house. The path runs level, turns a corner and descends a little, crossing a streambed. Climb past a couple of palms and turn round a corner to see one last caseta. Continue along the path, passing a few more palms in a little side-valley.

The path zigzags up a steep, scrubby, rocky slope, well-engineered, but rough and narrow. Follow it faithfully to reach a rugged gap at 833m (2733ft), where the village of Imada is seen at the head of the **Barranco de Guarimar**. Go straight across the gap as marked, turn right and contour above a few ruined houses. Cross a streambed in a valley at **Lasadoy**, zigzag up bare rock and turn a corner on red rock. Imada comes into view again.

Contour across the slope to reach a building, then descend and watch for markers while passing between terraces around the head of the barranco. Pass houses to reach a road-end in **Imada** where the PR LG 16.1 joins the PR LG 15. The Bar Cafeteria Arcilia is available, with a map-board nearby. ◄

Catch a bus to Alajeró and Playa de Santiago, or link with Walk 5.

WALK 5

Pajaritos to Playa de Santiago

Distance	15.5km (9½ miles)
Start	Pajaritos, Alto de Garajonay
Finish	Playa de Santiago
Total Ascent	75m (245ft)
Total Descent	1450m (4760ft)
Time	4hrs
Terrain	Some good tracks and paths, but also steep and rugged paths. Most of the route is downhill, but the optional ascent is a very steep climb.
Refreshment	Bar at Imada. Plenty of choice in Playa de Santiago. Bars at Alajeró on the optional route.
Transport	Buses serve Pajaritos from San Sebastián and Valle Gran Rey. Buses from Playa de Santiago serve San Sebastián, Alajeró and Valle Gran Rey.

This route starts high in the lush laurisilva on Alto de Garajonay and heads down to Imada. The splendidly scenic Barranco de Guarimar can be followed down to El Rumbazo for Playa de Santiago, though there is an option to climb instead to the villages of Targa and Alajeró.

Start at the road junction at **Pajaritos**, high on the forested slopes of Alto de Garajonay. Look for a sign for Los Roques, via Ruta 18 and GR 131, later flashed for the PR LG 15. The plain and obvious track leads to more signs, where a path on the left climbs a narrow groove on a forested slope. Log steps lead to a rocky summit. Walk down across a slight gap then up more log steps to a summit covered in cistus. The path heads down, undulating before dropping down more rugged terrain. There is always a road to the left but it is seldom seen. Land on a track and turn right as signposted for Imada,

Route uses PR LG 15, with an option to follow PR LG 15.1 and PR LG 15.2.

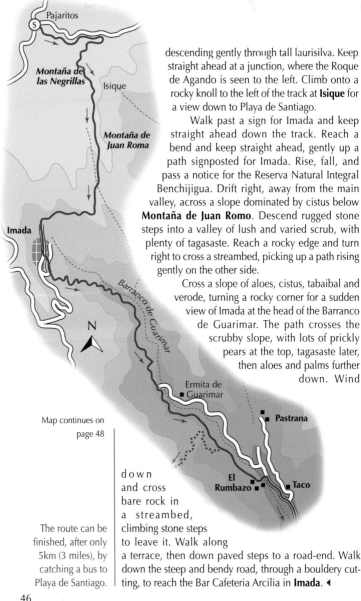

Pajaritos

Montaña de
las Negrillas

Isique

Montaña de
Juan Roma

Imada

Barranco de Guarimar

N

Ermita de
Guarimar

Pastrana

Map continues on
page 48

down
and cross
bare rock in
a streambed,

El
Rumbazo

Taco

The route can be
finished, after only
5km (3 miles), by
catching a bus to
Playa de Santiago.

descending gently through tall laurisilva. Keep straight ahead at a junction, where the Roque de Agando is seen to the left. Climb onto a rocky knoll to the left of the track at **Isique** for a view down to Playa de Santiago.

Walk past a sign for Imada and keep straight ahead down the track. Reach a bend and keep straight ahead, gently up a path signposted for Imada. Rise, fall, and pass a notice for the Reserva Natural Integral Benchijigua. Drift right, away from the main valley, across a slope dominated by cistus below **Montaña de Juan Romo**. Descend rugged stone steps into a valley of lush and varied scrub, with plenty of tagasaste. Reach a rocky edge and turn right to cross a streambed, picking up a path rising gently on the other side.

Cross a slope of aloes, cistus, tabaibal and verode, turning a rocky corner for a sudden view of Imada at the head of the Barranco de Guarimar. The path crosses the scrubby slope, with lots of prickly pears at the top, tagasaste later, then aloes and palms further down. Wind

climbing stone steps to leave it. Walk along a terrace, then down paved steps to a road-end. Walk down the steep and bendy road, through a bouldery cutting, to reach the Bar Cafeteria Arcilia in **Imada**. ◀

Walk down the road as signposted for Playa de Santiago, levelling out beside a small sports pitch. Turn left down steps, then right along a road to pass the Ermita de Santa Ana. Follow the road onwards, and while flights of steps descend to the left, only one of them is signposted as the PR LG 15. A stone-paved path runs down through the **Barranco de Guarimar**. Cross terraces and pass a ruin. ▶ The path runs down a soft band of rock then drops down smooth, bare rock, continuing along the valley side to pass an upstanding dyke. Turn a crumbling corner and look back to Imada for the last time.

Don't follow a level, easy path, but turn left down a winding, rocky path. Later, exploit a soft, red layer, heading downhill, uphill and across a rock-face, beneath an overhang. Next, a soft, yellow/creamy layer of rock leads steeply down across cliffs. A rugged path leads to a broken water channel; the path drops down a slope of aloes, prickly pears, tabaibal, verode and cistus. After following the path round a corner and further along its rugged course, palms grow on the way round a side-valley. Cross over and climb as flashed yellow/white, passing between houses to reach a track that leads down to a signpost. ▶

Walkers take in the view at the head of the Barranco de Guarimar near Imada

Huge boulders lie on slopes where palms and almonds grow.

The track offers a quick exit if needed.

47

Climb a narrow path signposted for El Rumbazo and Playa de Santiago. Cross a steep and rugged slope, passing a ruined caseta and another signpost. Keep left to head gradually down above another caseta. Look across the valley to see the **Ermita de Guarimar**. Pass lots of palms to reach a small building and a couple of ruins on old terraces. At this point choose between an easy descent to Playa de Santiago via the PR LG 15, or a steep climb up the PR LG 15.1 to Targa, then on to Antoncojo or Alajero (see later).

To Playa de Santiago

Keep straight ahead past the buildings and a few palms, up across a scrubby slope, then wind down past palms. The rugged path crosses scrubby slopes and a stone-paved path runs in front of houses at **El Rumbazo**. Go down stone steps and down a steep and bendy road to cross a bridge, reaching a road junction

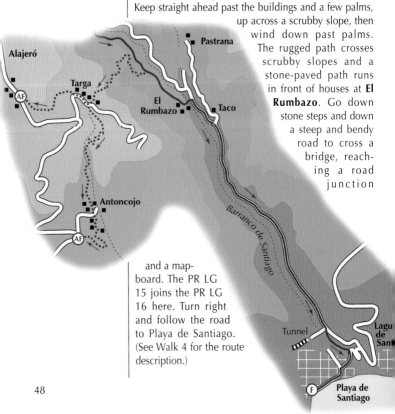

and a mapboard. The PR LG 15 joins the PR LG 16 here. Turn right and follow the road to Playa de Santiago. (See Walk 4 for the route description.)

Ascent to Targa

This is a steep and rocky climb of 500m (1640ft). Turn right to follow the PR LG 15.1 up a narrow, stone-paved path beside a barranco, passing palms. Cross the barranco and keep climbing, drifting right up a steep and scrubby buttress. Further uphill worn, red rock leads to a path junction. Turn left and climb across an old water channel, passing aloes, cistus, prickly pears, tabaibal and verode. The path climbs up around cliffs, in and out of gullies, exploiting every weakness to gain height on a formidable mountainside. The path is gentler as it crosses a rocky gap and reaches a road. Turn right up the road to a signpost at **Targa**, for options to walk to Alajeró or Antoncojo.

To Alajeró

Walk further along the road, step down to the left, cross a streambed, and climb back to the road. Cross the road and watch carefully for cairns and markers as the path is initially vague and rugged, though further uphill it is concrete. Turn left up a road to reach a little quarry on the right. Turn right just after the quarry to walk up a stone-paved path. Turn right across bare rock, then an

After a steep climb from the Barranco de Guarimar, Alajeró can be reached easily from Targa

See Walk 20 for
more information
about the GR132.

easy terrace path leads to an old house where a stone-paved path runs to the main road in **Alajeró**. The Bar Restaurante Las Palmeras is across the road and the GR 132 runs nearby. ◄

To Antoncojo

This route runs downhill, around 300m (985ft). Leave **Targa** as signposted for Antoncojo, crossing bare rock and following a narrow path between low walls across old terraces, past a few palms. Climb a little then keep right at a path junction as marked. A rugged path zigzags down a slope of aloes, cistus, asphodel and prickly pears, to the rocky bed of a barranco. Do not cross, but head downstream, scrambling on rock if necessary. A scanty path appears, and a boulder threatens to push walkers into the stream, but still do not cross. Step up onto a terrace, then down a terrace, then turn right and left and finally cross the streambed.

The path runs uphill and is obvious, but rugged underfoot. There is a slight rise to cross an old water channel then it runs down, passing above a small reservoir, staying close to a cliff. Walk towards houses at **Antoncojo**, following the path and a road down to a junction. Turn right down the road to another junction. At this point, a right turn leads up to the main road, while a left turn leads gently down to a GR 132 signpost. Turning right at this point leads up a stone-paved road to the main road, a map-board and bus shelter.

WALK 6

Chipude and Barranco de Argaga

Distance	10km (6¼ miles)
Start	Chipude
Finish	Vueltas, Valle Gran Rey
Total Ascent	40m (130ft)
Total Descent	1100m (3610ft)
Time	3hrs 30min
Terrain	Gentle roads and paths, followed by steep and rugged paths, then hands-on scrambling in a steep and rocky barranco. Easy tracks at the end.
Refreshment	Bars at Chipude and Valle Gran Rey.
Transport	Buses from San Sebastián and Playa de Santiago link Chipude and Valle Gran Rey.

The Barranco de Argaga starts as a gentle valley near Chipude, becoming very steep and rocky on the way to the sea near Valle Gran Rey. Most people climb it, but the descent is easier. Whatever direction is chosen, this is a tough hands-on scramble requiring a head for heights.

Leave the church and plaza in **Chipude**, around 1060m (3480ft), and walk a short way down the road. Turn left as signposted for the PR LG 14 for Valle Gran Rey. Follow the road, turn right at a junction and down to a **cemetery**. Keep left to follow a path gently uphill, past tabaibal, prickly pears and aloes. Drop down to cross a road at a house, and continue down to keep right of another house, following a rugged path down a slope of prickly pears. Swing left along a terrace and go down bare red rock to a road bend at **Guarchico**.

Turn right to walk gently up the road, almost to a junction, but turn left along a path flashed yellow/white, later passing a small building among narrow fields. Wind

Route uses PR LG 14.

gently downhill and keep straight ahead at a junction at the base of a pylon. At another junction beside a tumbled ruin, turn left down a boulder-paved path. Cross a road and go down an easy path, becoming

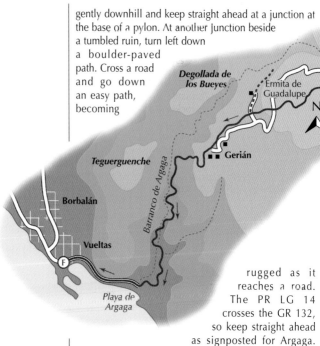

Degollada de los Bueyes

Ermita de Guadalupe

N

Teguerguenche

Barranco de Argaga

Gerián

Borbalán

Vueltas

F

Playa de Argaga

rugged as it reaches a road. The PR LG 14 crosses the GR 132, so keep straight ahead as signposted for Argaga. Reach the edge of a barranco to follow the path and an old water channel to houses at **Gerián**, around 730m (2395ft). Avoid the road until you have to step onto it at a signpost.

The PR LG 14 runs along the edge of the barranco, past a building to reach aloes on a broad, stony area. Turn right to pass a notice for the Parque Rural Valle Gran Rey. The path descends gently and easily, then becomes steep and rugged on crumbling beds of red ash and pumice. There are palms to the right, pines to the left and aloes and bare rock further down. The path is broken just before a palm and this might cause confusion, so don't go down past it, but pick up a terrace path across the slope. Later, drop down to another terrace and follow a fence past more palms, a steep and rugged descent. A narrow path cuts into a cliff and hands must be used to get down steep steps onto an easy terrace, deep in the **Barranco de Argaga**, around 400m (1310ft).

A rocky path traverses round a bend. Beware a gaping hole and go down the path, then down a short, steep, stack of stone steps against a buttress. Turn left along

The Barranco de Argaga is steep and rocky throughout its length and needs care

53

a rugged terrace and pass beneath an overhang and a water pipe. Markers later show a way down to the right, traversing back across the slope to go down awkward steps against rocky buttresses. Pass the water pipe again and follow a narrow traverse with cliffs above and below, with wet and greasy slabs. Steep and rocky zigzags drop from ledge to ledge, passing beneath an overhang. Drop down to land in the rocky bed of the barranco.

Continue downstream, passing under the water pipe again, and cross the rocky bed of the barranco above a normally dry waterfall. Follow an easy path dropping from terrace to terrace then walk down the bed of the barranco to reach the lip of another dry waterfall. Cross the barranco as marked to pick up a path on a slope. Climb steeply and ruggedly, contour and pass beneath an overhang. The descent back into the barranco is steep and stony. Watch for markers and go down rock steps towards the bottom to land on a flat terrace.

Cross the streambed and pick up a path on the other side. This runs easily above a deep gorge cut into ash and pumice. Cross a dam to reach large terraces supported by massive walls, and drop down beside them. Go through a narrow gorge and keep left of a dammed pool. The path drops and continues down the barranco, switching from side to side. Cross to the right-hand side to pass beneath a footbridge. Continue down the bouldery bed among cane thickets to reach a track.

Walk down the track, passing a tropical fruit garden, crossing the barranco from side to side, eventually reaching a bouldery beach at **Playa de Argaga**. Turn right along a dirt road below sheer cliffs that have a habit of dropping stones and boulders without warning. Calle El Carmen leads to a roundabout at the port of **Vueltas**, where there are bars and restaurants.

WALK 7
Chipude and La Matanza

Distance	5 or 7.5km (3 or 4½ miles)
Start/Finish	Chipude.
Alternative Finish	El Guro, Valle Gran Rey
Total Ascent/Descent	350m (1150ft)
Time	2hrs 45min or 3hrs 30min
Terrain	Mostly good paths and tracks dropping into and climbing from a valley full of terraces.
Refreshment	Bars at Chipude and El Cercado.
Transport	Buses link Chipude and El Cercado with Valle Gran Rey, San Sebastián, Playa de Santiago and Vallehermoso.

Leaving the upland village of Chipude this short walk drops down to La Matanza and climbs to El Cercado, where an easy walk leads back to Chipude. There is an option to head further downhill from La Matanza, joining the GR 132 to descend to Valle Gran Rey.

Leave the church and plaza in Chipude, around 1060m (3480ft), and walk down the road. The PR LG 14 is signposted off to the left, but stay on the main road, round a right-hand bend, watching for another signpost on the left, the PR LG 13 for La Matanza. Walk down the road and turn right down a few steps, then left along a narrow terrace path. Pass between two houses and walk down to a track and a signpost. (The route returns here later.)

Turn left a little, then right to continue along a narrow path across terraces, contouring, even rising a little, but generally heading downhill. Little houses are tucked away deep in the valley. Pass an outcrop of rock and zigzag down into the **Barranco de La Matanza** as flashed yellow/white, avoiding other paths. Reach the streambed

Route uses PR LG 13, with an option to follow PR LG 13.2 and GR 132.

The whitewashed church and the central plaza in the upland village of Chipude

among palms and tabaibal, around 785m (2575ft), at a signpost. Either turn right to climb to El Cercado, or turn left to follow another route finishing at Valle Gran Rey (see later).

Cross the stream at **La Matanza** and turn right for El Cercado. Climb a rugged stony path, passing a hut in a cave. Climb past terraces covered in tabaibal, prickly pears and aloes, levelling out beside a couple of palms. Climb and level out again and again, reaching a streambed in a side-valley. Climb a gently-graded path with a view of El Cercado above. Keep left of the streambed then later cross to the right and climb further. Houses and a road are reached at **El Cercado**, over 1000m (3280ft). Divert off-route to reach bars and pottery shops.

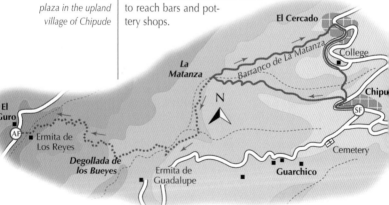

Turn right along a road, passing the last houses in the village, heading up towards a **college**. Keep straight ahead and go down a winding, stone-paved path, rugged underfoot and flanked by walls. Cross the valley and follow a track to reach a signpost that was passed earlier in the day. Simply turn left and follow the path uphill to return to **Chipude**.

Optional Descent to Valle Gran Rey

This route allows a linear walk from Chipude to Valle Gran Rey and El Guro, worth considering if the higher parts are misty, while the sun shines far below. The full descent is around 900m (2950ft).

Leave **La Matanza** as signposted for the PR LG 13.2. The path is easy and follows a broken water channel past a small building. The slopes are covered in aloes, prickly pears and almonds. Enter a side-valley and cross a rocky streambed. Continue onwards as the slope steepens and walk in the old water channel at times. The path links with the course of the GR 132, which is signposted down to the right for **Valle Gran Rey**. ▶

See Walk 21 for the route description.

Following the PR LG 13.2 from La Matanza to link with the GR 132 to Valle Gran Rey

WALK 8

La Laguna Grande and Alto de Garajonay

Distance	11km (7 miles)
Start/Finish	La Laguna Grande
Total Ascent/Descent	400m (1310ft)
Time	4hrs
Terrain	Mostly along good tracks and paths, though careful route finding is needed at frequent junctions in dense forest.
Refreshment	Bar restaurant at La Laguna Grande.
Transport	None for La Laguna Grande; buses link Pajaritos with San Sebastián, Chipude and Valle Gran Rey.

This walk is in the heart of the Parque Nacional de Garajonay, where paths and tracks in dense laurisilva forest are marked with distinctive green signs. This figure-of-eight route starts from La Laguna Grande and takes in the highest point on La Gomera, Alto de Garajonay.

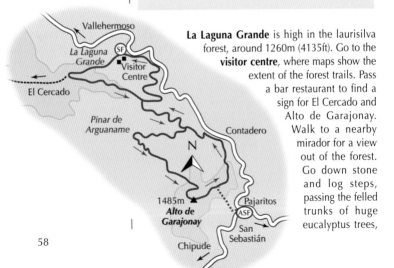

La Laguna Grande is high in the laurisilva forest, around 1260m (4135ft). Go to the **visitor centre**, where maps show the extent of the forest trails. Pass a bar restaurant to find a sign for El Cercado and Alto de Garajonay. Walk to a nearby mirador for a view out of the forest. Go down stone and log steps, passing the felled trunks of huge eucalyptus trees,

reaching the edge of the forest at a 'limite del parque' notice.

Turn left up a track, where the laurisilva is outgrown by tall pines, and later tall chestnuts. However, the laurisilva becomes tall and dense further uphill. Reach a track where Alto de Garajonay is signposted to the right as Ruta 14. ▶ Follow the track gently down and round a bend to another junction. Turn left uphill and note how more stout eucalyptus trees have been felled. When the next junction is reached, turn right for Ruta 14, follow the track down round a bend then climb a more steeply than before. There is a brief glimpse of the rugged Fortaleza de Cherelepín away to the right.

Reach a junction with a path, where a left turn is signposted for Alto de Garajonay and Ruta 14. Follow the path up through dense heather, climbing lots of log steps. Continue gently along a crest where there are views between trees and bushy scrub. Alto de Garajonay rises ahead, while La Fortaleza is away to the right. When a fork is reached, head left down into dense forest. Emerge on a track and turn left uphill. A steep climb leads to

La Laguna Grande, which really does become a shallow lagoon after a period of heavy rain

Watch for more signs with this number.

another junction. Turn left to reach yet another junction. Turn right up the track and follow it round a broad bend to reach another junction. Turn left to follow one last track and a stone-paved path to the summit of **Alto de Garajonay** at 1485m (4872ft).

Alto de Garajonay is the highest point on La Gomera and a splendid viewpoint. Lush, green laurisilva spreads in all directions. The towering forms of El Teide and Guajara are seen on Tenerife, with El Hierro and La Palma also in view. On misty days nothing is visible, though it is interesting to see how much moisture the 'cloud forest' can sieve from the air, dripping constantly onto the ground.

Looking from the summit of Alto de Garajonay to the neighbouring summit of La Fortaleza

Garajonay was the last refuge for the native Guanches in 1489. Their territorial boundaries met on the summit and it was held in high regard. The circular stone enclosure is a replica of a ritual structure which was excavated, then re-interred. Large quantities of sheep and goat bones were discovered, as well as stone implements.

Leave Alto de Garajonay down a flight of steps and follow a path signposted for Contadero. Head gently down the heathery crest, then steeply down log steps to a path junction on a gap. ▶ Cross the gap and climb log steps, continuing along the heathery crest to a junction, turning left for Contadero. Look out for a couple of miradores on the right. The path is more rugged as it winds down log steps to a track. Follow the track downhill, reaching a pronounced right bend above a road at **Contadero**.

The route can be re-structured to start and finish here, linking with buses serving Pajaritos.

Turn left as signposted for La Laguna Grande and Ruta 14, down a narrow path with log steps into dense laurisilva. ▶ Pass a roadside parking space and walk ahead down a bendy track for La Laguna Grande. Dense forest gives way to an open area at a junction. Keep straight ahead gently down the bendy track, reaching another junction where stout eucalyptus trees have been felled. (This track was used earlier in the day.)

The path runs parallel to the road and there are views back to the high forested crest.

Walk ahead along the track, go round a bend and slightly uphill to another junction, and keep ahead again to climb uphill, as signposted for La Laguna Grande and Ruta 14. The track leads up to the road and more signs. Follow a narrow path parallel to the road, and when they part company, go down log steps to return to **La Laguna Grande**.

WALK 9

El Cercado and Valle Gran Rey

Distance	8km (5 miles)
Start/Finish	El Cercado
Alternative Finish	El Guro, Valle Gran Rey
Total Ascent/Descent	600m (1970ft)
Time	5hrs
Terrain	Steep and often rugged stone-paved paths, downhill and uphill.
Refreshment	Bars at El Cercado. Bars off-route in Valle Gran Rey and a bar at El Guro.
Transport	Buses link El Cercado and El Guro with San Sebastián and Playa de Santiago.

El Cercado stands high above Valle Gran Rey, and a casual glance at the steep and rugged slopes separating them suggests that they cannot be linked. In fact, there are two steep, winding, stone-paved paths that link to make an arduous circular walk there-and-back.

Route uses PR LG 12, with options to follow PR LG 12.1 and PR LG 12.2.

Start in El Cercado, around 1020m (3345ft), at a road bend opposite the Bar Maria. A signpost for Valle Gran Rey points along a road. Walk along and down the road on a high crest, passing a few houses, then rising towards a hump. However, turn right as signposted, passing a notice for the Parque Rural Valle Gran Rey, following a path that contours or descends gently, overlooking the deep, steep-sided **Barranco del Agua**.

Palms and houses spread throughout the valley, while the bongling bells of sheep and goats are heard.

Crumbling steps on red pumice give way to stone steps winding downhill. The path wanders across steep slopes between cliffs, zigzagging through breaches, with views over Valle Gran Rey. ◀ A long flight of rebuilt steps drop down a steep slope of palms and terraces. A zigzag stone-paved 'street' runs down past houses to reach a road and map-board at **La Vizcaina**, where a shop and bar are available nearby.

For an easy finish, turn left down the road as signposted for Valle Gran Rey (see later). To walk back up to El Cercado, turn right up the road. Pass houses and pass masses of vegetation while crossing the **Barranco del Agua**. The road reaches more houses at **Lomo del Balo** and a signpost points right for El Cercado. ▶

Climb stone steps with handrails, zigzagging up past houses, watching for yellow/white flashes. Rugged stone steps climb steeply to the last buildings, or wooden cabins. A rugged stone-paved path climbs steeply and directly with views back over Valle Gran Rey. The slopes are covered in tabaibal, verode, prickly pears, aloes, broom, cornical, incienso and palms. There is a distinct drift left, then a sharp turn right as stone steps climb higher and higher. The path levels out to exploit a soft layer of rock, then zigzags steeply uphill, back and forth beneath a pylon line. There is abundant tagasaste towards the top of the boulder-paved path and the gradient eases at a signpost. The path undulates along **Lomo de La Laja**, past low tagasaste, heather trees and cistus, leaving the Parque Rural Valle Gran Rey. Keep climbing gently to

The road onwards is the PR LG 12.1, climbing to the Bar Macondo, reaching the main road at the head of Valle Gran Rey.

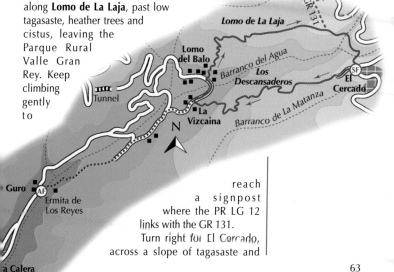

reach a signpost where the PR LG 12 links with the GR 131. Turn right for El Cercado, across a slope of tagasaste and

The gradient eases on the ascent, once Lomo de La Laja has been reached

cistus, and go down a boulder-paved zigzag. A level path runs beneath an overhang, with the barranco falling below. Drop down past terraces, cross a streambed, and contour across a terrace with a view down to Valle Gran Rey. Cross another streambed and climb winding stone steps on a slope of cistus, tagasaste and heather trees. A road bend is reached at the Bar Maria in **El Cercado**, where the walk began. Traditional pottery shops operate nearby.

To Valle Gran Rey and El Guro

This avoids the 600m (1970ft) climb to El Cercado, dropping almost 320m (1050ft) through the valley instead. Turn left down the road to leave **La Vizcaina**, passing a shop and a bar, houses, palms and terraces. The road narrows as it passes between more houses, reaching a hairpin bend. Turn left, in effect straight ahead, down to a road-end where there might be a café. Go down stone steps and a stone-paved path. Pass a couple of houses and follow a rugged path across a slope of pumice, passing a couple more houses. A slight ascent reaches

a junction, so keep ahead for the **Ermita de Los Reyes** and its little plaza. Walk down stone-paved steps into the barranco and cross its bouldery bed and a track. Follow a stone-paved path through cane thickets and climb stone steps with railings to the main road at **El Guro** in Valle Gran Rey, where a shop and bar are available.

The Ermita de Los Reyes is passed on a variant route down through Valle Gran Rey

WALK 10

Las Hayas, Arure and Valle Gran Rey

Distance	12km (7½ miles)
Start	Las Hayas
Finish	La Calera, Valle Gran Rey
Total Ascent	190m (625ft)
Total Descent	1130m (3710ft)
Time	4hrs
Terrain	Easy roads, tracks and paths, ending with a very steep and rugged descent.
Refreshment	Bars at Las Hayas, Arure and off-route in Valle Gran Rey.
Transport	Buses serve Las Hayas, Arure and Valle Gran Rey from San Sebastián and Playa de Santiago.

A simple walk along roads, tracks and paths links the villages of Las Hayas and Arure. The route can be continued along the upland crest of La Mérica, following a popular path that ends by zigzagging down a very steep slope to La Calera at the foot of Valle Gran Rey.

Route uses PR LG 11 and GR 132.

Start at a crossroads at Las Hayas, around 1000m (3280ft), where there is a map-board below the Restaurante La Montaña. Follow the road signposted to Arure, downhill a little, then turn right up another road. Head down past a cultivated area; then the road is flanked by heather trees, reaching a fork. Keep right and climb uphill, passing low laurisilva on red earth. Cross a hump and walk downhill, keeping straight ahead at a junction to go up the road. At the end of the road a track on the right is signposted for Arure, dropping to become a winding, deeply-grooved path. Emerge from the forest at the bottom and follow a road through a gentle, cultivated valley.

Keep straight ahead and downhill at all junctions, passing to the right of a reservoir to reach a main road.

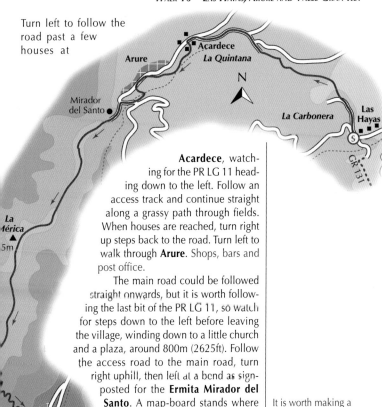

Turn left to follow the road past a few houses at

Acardece, watching for the PR LG 11 heading down to the left. Follow an access track and continue straight along a grassy path through fields. When houses are reached, turn right up steps back to the road. Turn left to walk through **Arure**. Shops, bars and post office.

The main road could be followed straight onwards, but it is worth following the last bit of the PR LG 11, so watch for steps down to the left before leaving the village, winding down to a little church and a plaza, around 800m (2625ft). Follow the access road to the main road, turn right uphill, then left at a bend as signposted for the **Ermita Mirador del Santo**. A map-board stands where the PR LG 11 joins the GR 132. ▶

It is worth making a detour to the *mirador*.

Keep straight ahead as signposted for Valle Gran Rey. The road ends suddenly and there is a view down into the valley. Continue along a dirt road, rising and falling, keeping left at a fork to pass a notice for the Parque Rural Valle Gran Rey. Follow the track down a little, then uphill, keeping right as signposted up a stone-paved ramp. The path crosses a water channel and passes a goat pen. Cross a rocky notch and descend a little, overlooking the head of Valle Gran Rey.

View from the village of Arure, on the way to the church, with the crest of La Mérica beyond

Zigzag uphill, pass a cave, and keep climbing the broad path while enjoying widening views.

The descent starts as the path passes close to **La Mérica**, whose summit rises to 835m (2740ft). The ground is remarkably bright, especially in full sun. Exhausted terraces flank the path and even the scrub seems parched. There is a view over the edge into Valle Gran Rey, and ruins are passed beside an old limekiln. The broad path drops gradually to pass another old building and an *era*, or circular threshing floor. Keep walking down until a fork is reached.

Turn left and be sure to pick up and follow a path that zigzags more and more steeply downhill. The path is often paved, but is also rugged and covered in loose stones. The last stretch features excellent paving and a flight of steps drops onto a narrow road at **La Calera**. Turn right down the road and wind down through narrow streets and alleys to reach a couple of bars and shops on the main road. Taxis park here and a bus station is located nearby.

WALK 11

Vallehermoso to Chorros de Epina

Distance	11km (7 miles)
Start	Vallehermoso
Finish	Chorros de Epina
Total Ascent	800m (2625ft)
Total Descent	180m (590ft)
Time	4hrs
Terrain	Mostly good paths and tracks, with some steep slopes and forest. Optional steep descent to the coast.
Refreshment	Plenty of choice in Vallehermoso. Bar at Chorros de Epina.
Transport	Buses link Vallehermoso and Chorros de Epina with Chipude and Alojera.

The PR LG 10 leaves Vallehermoso, climbs up through a barranco into laurisilva, reaching the the Ermita de Santa Clara. An optional path runs down through Arguamul to the coast. Easy tracks and paths can be followed to Chorros de Epina, where there are buses back to Vallehermoso.

Start in the centre of Vallehermoso, where a four-way signpost shows routes out of the plaza. For the PR LG 10, leave the plaza via the Bar Restaurante Pensión Central and Bar Cafetería Chamire. Turn left up steps, then right up more steps to a road. Turn right down the road, which bends left. Turn left as signposted for the PR LG 10, up to a cemetery. Step down to the right and follow a path across a valley. Climb a winding, stone-paved path past a few houses and go a little further up a slope dotted with junipers, levelling out on a path fringed with aloes. Pass a ruin and climb gently into the **Barranco de la Era Nueva**. ▸

Pass a caseta and notice how the mixed scrub becomes denser. Later, climb above a concrete tank,

Route uses PR LG 10, with an option to follow PR LG 10.1.

Palms grow on the valley floor, with junipers on the slopes.

69

drop a little, rise gently and cross a small *era*, or thresh-ing floor. While wandering through thickets of cane after-wards, cross the bed of the barranco and continue past tall scrub. The path becomes narrow and brambly, then stone-paved as it winds uphill and laurisilva begins to develop. Climb a groove worn in soft, crumbling bed-rock, passing a couple of eucalyptus trees to reach a shoulder of bare earth.

A rocky path climbs through laurisilva to reach a fenced edge. Traverse easily across a steep slope, passing another fenced edge to reach a track, map-board and signposts near the **Ermita de Santa Clara**, around 735m (2410ft). Either turn left to follow the track signposted for Epina, or cross the track to pick up a path leading downhill, signposted PR LG 10.1 (see later).

The track slices across a steep, forested slope, generally run-ning gently downhill past **La Caldera**, with views of the coast. Keep right at a junction, crossing slopes covered in fragrant

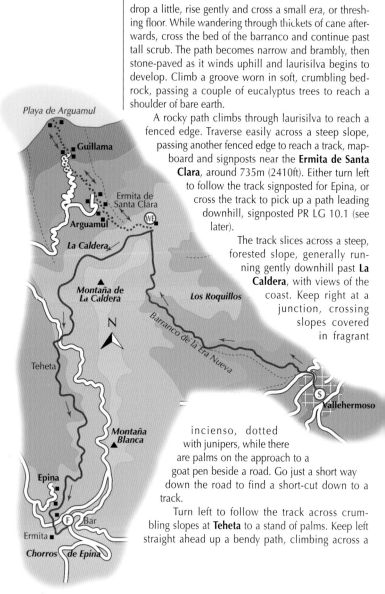

incienso, dotted with junipers, while there are palms on the approach to a goat pen beside a road. Go just a short way down the road to find a short-cut down to a track.

Turn left to follow the track across crum-bling slopes at **Teheta** to a stand of palms. Keep left straight ahead up a bendy path, climbing across a

slope dotted with junipers and broom. The path wanders in and out of side-valleys where palms grow, later climbing a grassy, bushy slope before making a short, steep, rocky descent. Traverse a slope of palms, passing terraces and walk between crumbling casetas. Watch for yellow/white markers, or keep straight ahead at a junction, generally rising to reach concrete steps.

The Ermita de Santa Clara stands at 735m (2410ft)

Turn left up the steps to a road. Turn right and quickly left to climb steep and winding steps to another road. Cross over and follow a winding path up through mixed woodland to reach a junction with the GR 132. Either turn right to see a curious spring, returning afterwards, or climb stone steps to reach an **ermita**. Either way, follow the GR 132 as signposted for Vallehermoso, up a wooded slope to reach a road around 800m (2625ft). Turn left for the Restaurante Los Chorros de Epina and catch a bus back to Vallehermoso. ▶

Or follow Walk 22 back to Vallehermoso via the GR 132.

Stories are told about the spring at **Chorros de Epina**, which issues from seven spouts. In order for women to find their true love, they should drink from the even-numbered spouts, counting from the left, while men should drink from the odd-numbered spouts. Women who drink from the odd-numbered spouts will become witches!

Optional Extension to Playa de Arguamul

This extension drops steeply, measures 3km (2 miles) one-way, with a descent of 735m (2410ft). Bear in mind that the return route will be a very steep ascent!

Start near the **Ermita de Santa Clara**, as signposted for the PR LG 10.1. A path winds down a grassy slope between patchy laurisilva. It later swings left to make a falling traverse, reaching a small white hut. A winding, stone-paved path runs down a slope of aromatic incienso. Go past palms in a ravine, then aloes, then drop down a slope of tabaibal to reach houses at **Arguamul**. Follow a stone-paved path downhill and down steps, reaching a narrow road.

Cross the road to continue down steps below a house, then straight ahead along a narrow path, past terraces of vines and palms. Cross a track and walk down a rugged, stone-paved path, keeping right to avoid a house. Walk along a level terrace and head downhill, keeping right of another house. The path has a water pipe on the right and later a huge stone wall on the left. Walk in front of a house and go down a concrete path to a road. Walk down the very bendy road, passing prickly pears, calcosas, taibabal and verode, to reach the Capilla de Santa Clara.

Follow a concrete path up and down through the tiny village of **Guillama**. Turn right down a path, then after passing cultivated plots, turn left down past old terraces. Tabaibilla grows on rocky slopes, while further downhill uvillas grow among sparse scrub. Head for a huddle of old buildings and go in front of the one closest to the sea to find a path down to a bouldery beach. Retrace the route all the way back up to the **Ermita de Santa Clara**.

A path descends steep slopes on the optional route down past Arguamul to the rugged coast

WALK 12
Vallehermoso and Cumbre de Chijeré

Distance	13km (8 miles)
Start/Finish	Vallehermoso
Total Ascent/Descent	740m (2425ft)
Time	4hrs
Terrain	Mostly along good paths and tracks, but the paths are sometimes steep and rugged.
Refreshment	Plenty of choice in Vallehermoso.
Transport	Buses serve Vallehermoso from San Sebastián, Hermigua, Chipude and Alojera.

> This route encircles the Barranco de los Guanches, climbing onto the Cumbre de Chijeré. There is an option to extend it to the Ermita de Santa Clara, or simply descend by way of Lomo San Pedro. The whole area is noted for its abundance of junipers, or *sabinas*.

Route uses PR LG 9 and GR 131, with options to follow PR LG 9.1 and PR LG 9.2.

Start in the centre of **Vallehermoso**, where a four-way signpost shows routes out of the plaza. For the PR LG 9, leave the plaza and walk down to the little bus station, turning right down the road signposted for the Parque Marítimo. Walk down the road to a bend to find a GR 131 signpost on the right. Go down a short, stone-paved path and turn left at the bottom, down a narrow and well-vegetated path. Cross a streambed and look for combined red/yellow/white markers on rocks, walls and pipes. These reveal a narrow path heading gently down through the valley, passing between cultivated terraces on a steep slope. Most of the time there is a water pipe alongside.

When a path junction is reached, keep left to follow the GR 131, zigzagging down to a lower path, turning round a side-valley, the Barranco de la Culata. Join a narrow road past a few houses and follow it as it drops more

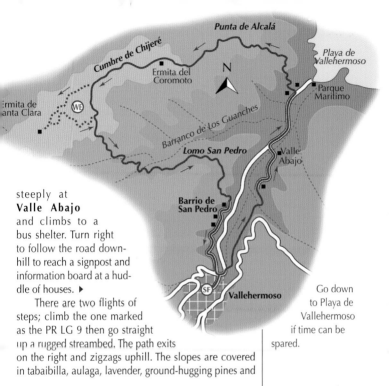

steeply at
Valle Abajo
and climbs to a
bus shelter. Turn right
to follow the road down-
hill to reach a signpost and
information board at a huddle of houses. ▶

There are two flights of
steps; climb the one marked
as the PR LG 9 then go straight
up a rugged streambed. The path exits
on the right and zigzags uphill. The slopes are covered
in tabaibilla, aulaga, lavender, ground-hugging pines and

Go down
to Playa de
Vallehermoso
if time can be
spared.

A short detour down the road allows a visit to Playa de Vallehermoso

junipers. The path drifts right as it climbs, overlooking the cliff coast. Climb past squat trees, generally up a rocky ridge. As the path moves away from the cliffs the trees become taller and the gradient eases. A track is reached near **Punta de Alcalá**, around 560m (1840ft).

Turn left to follow the track for Santa Clara along the **Cumbre de Chijeré**. Eroded slopes are being re-forested and are dotted with junipers, heather trees, pines, calcosas and incienso. Keep left at a track junction and walk up past the **Ermita del Coromoto**. Coloured earth is strewn with boulders and gullies have been dammed to prevent further erosion. The track reaches a signpost where a path on the right allows an extension to the **Ermita de Santa Clara**. To stay on the main route, just follow the track until a signpost points left for Vallehermoso.

Optional Extension to Santa Clara

An optional extension leads quickly and easily to the Ermita de Santa Clara

This adds only 1.5km (1 mile) to the route. Turn right to follow the PR LG 9.1 for Santa Clara. It wanders along or close to a worn crest, overlooking a steep slope of laurisilva and the rugged coast. Follow it to the **Ermita de Santa**

Clara, around 735m (2410ft). Turn left to follow a track signposted as the PR LG 9.2, winding across a forested slope, joining the main route where another track drops to the right.

The track runs downhill, clearly marked and signposted, becoming a path along a ridge of sparse laurisilva, juniper and incienso. Go through a little gate and wind down a groove on a steep slope. Go through another little gate and the path cuts down across a steep slope, then winds down past junipers. Walk further down a steep slope, passing lots of aloes and a little house. Watch for markers while passing terraces to cross the bed of the barranco.

A path rises gently across a steep slope. Turn right round a rocky corner and head down into another barranco. Cross it and climb, then follow a rising traverse across a steep terraced slope, mostly covered in grass and tabaibal. The path drops gently across a steep slope of junipers, then rises across a steep slope to reach another corner, where there is a lot of tabaibilla. Enjoy views from **Lomo San Pedro**, follow a rugged path downhill, then a gentle falling traverse across a slope of junipers. The path is rough and broken round a little valley.

Don't go left down to nearby houses, but watch for a marked right turn and continue across a slope of junipers. Go down winding concrete steps from a house to a road. Turn right up the road, which is bendy and undulating, running parallel to the main road in the valley. This quiet route runs through the **Barrio de San Pedro**, joining the main road in **Vallehermoso**. Walk past the little bus station to return to the centre of town.

WALK 13
Vallehermoso and Los Loros

Distance	14km (8¾ miles)
Start/Finish	Vallehermoso
Total Ascent/Descent	800m (2625ft)
Time	4hrs 30min
Terrain	Easy roads and tracks, along with some steep, narrow and sometimes overgrown paths on slopes of scrub and forest.
Refreshment	Plenty of choice in Vallehermoso.
Transport	Buses serve Vallehermoso from San Sebastián, Hermigua, Chipude and Alojera.

This route uses part of the GR 131 to climb from Vallehermoso into the laurisilva cloud forest on the fringes of the national park. It then works its way round forested valleys before descending, passing lots of small settlements and intricate cultivated areas along the way.

Route includes PR LG 8 and GR 131.

Start in the centre of **Vallehermoso**, where a four-way signpost shows routes out of the plaza. For the PR LG 8 and GR 131, leave from the plaza via the post office (Correos), and

A fine view down through the Vallehermoso from near La Vistita del Rosario

refer to the route description in Walk 26 to reach a gap, at **La Vistita del Rosario**, where the GR 131 climbs onwards, while the PR LG 8 turns left downhill.

Descend using a steep path winding down past a bewildering range of plants and bushy scrub, while patchy laurisilva tries to compete. Pass a waymark post and head down to a road bend and map-board. Turning left allows a short-cut down through **Los Loros**, but turn right to follow the road uphill as signposted. Tarmac gives way to a broad track rising across wooded slopes. Avoid a track down to a small reservoir, and keep climbing the main track. There is a dip further along, before the track crosses a wooded, brambly streambed. Keep climbing to reach a bend at **Cruz de las Animas**, around 725m (2380ft), where there is a shrine and signpost for the PR LG 8.

Turn left to follow an easy path along a forested crest. Steps later drop to one side or the other of the crest, either worn or stone-paved, reaching a signpost. Keep walking ahead, down through laurisilva, which gives way to terraces and vines on the way down to a stream. Turn right towards houses, cross a concrete slab and continue downstream, then climb to a road.

Walk down the road through the valley, passing lots of houses, farms and cultivated areas. The road only climbs a little as it passes above a **reservoir**, Presa de la Encantadora. ▶ Pass a map-board near the access road for the dam and keep following the road. After turning a pronounced bend at **Los Chapines**, it is simply a matter of retracing the earliest steps of the day, back down the road to **Vallehermoso**.

A road can be followed on the other side, linking with Walk 14.

WALK 14

Vallehermoso and El Tión

Distance	9km (5½ miles)
Start/Finish	Vallehermoso
Total Ascent/Descent	500m (1640ft)
Time	3hrs 15min
Terrain	Easy roads and tracks then steep, narrow and occasionally overgrown paths on forested slopes.
Refreshment	Plenty of choice in Vallehermoso.
Transport	Buses serve Vallehermoso from San Sebastián, Hermigua, Chipude and Alojera.

This route makes an interesting circuit from Vallehermoso, high above the cultivated and forested slopes of the Barranco del Ingenio. It could also be used as an alternative to the GR 132 from Vallehermoso, climbing through the barranco and using a variant spur to re join the trail.

Route uses PR LG 7, with an option to follow PR LG 7.1.

Start in the centre of Vallehermoso, where a four-way signpost shows routes out of the plaza. For the PR LG 7, leave from the plaza and walk down the main road, as signposted for Garabato. Turn right, again signposted for Garabato. Walk up the road and keep left at a junction, up round a bend, turning right up concrete steps. Turn right up a road to reach a junction and signpost. The GR 132 turns left, but walk straight ahead up the road to follow the PR LG 7 for El Tión. The gradient eases as it becomes a concrete road passing a few houses, and a track continues up through the valley. There are terraces in the valley bottom at **Garabato**, with forested mountains ahead.

The track is very convoluted, crossing the valley bottom and climbing up the other side. There are more houses high in the valley, as well as terraces and palms, but the slopes now feature laurisilva and cistus. Keep climbing the bendy track, noting the dam of the Presa de Garabato **reservoir** ahead. Before reaching it, turn sharp right as signposted for El Tión.

A path has been hacked from a steep rib of soft, yellow rock with crude stone steps zigzagging uphill. The forest is quite mixed, with trees and bushes.

A path hammered from a rocky ridge on the highest part of the route

81

The view back down into the valley from high on the forested slopes near Roque Blanco

Enjoy views back to Vallehermoso and across to Roque Cano.

Towards the top, the path has been hammered out of a rocky rib, climbing to little buildings around 600m (1970ft). ◄ Either turn right, signposted PR LG 7 for Ambrosio, or if wishing to join the GR 132, turn left as signposted PR LG 7.1 (see later).

Turning right the path becomes very narrow, following a water channel across a slope, entering dense woodland with trailing brambles. This is awkward, but persevere to reach a rocky rib and fine valley views. An easy rising traverse leads through dense woods to a gap behind **Roque Blanco**, where heather trees, tagasaste and cistus grow. Follow the path as it winds down a narrow, steep, worn groove. It becomes overgrown so watch carefully for turnings on the way down to a narrow road.

Walking across the dam links with Walk 13.

Turn right to follow the bendy road downhill, passing houses and terraces, overlooking the reservoir of Presa de la Encantadora. Further down, the road bends sharp left, but keep right, or straight ahead, along a track as signposted. Reach the **reservoir** dam and walk down steps towards it. ◄ Turn right and walk along a path, away from the dam, following a pipeline up into a valley past cistus scrub. Don't follow the pipe across the valley, but keep to a narrow, winding, overgrown path up to an intersection of paths on a gentle gap.

Roque Cano is straight ahead and a path follows a black plastic pipe in that direction. Swing left down onto the rounded, scrubby crest of Lomo Pelado, where bits of broken water channel might be noticed. The path crosses from side to side down the crest, sometimes in patchy woodland. The way ahead becomes increasingly rugged, so watch for a path zigzagging down to the left, on a rugged slope of mixed scrub. A concrete path passes a few houses, with fine views of Vallehermoso. Follow a tarmac road winding downhill and pass between two reservoirs. Walk up to the Hotel de Triana and down into the centre of Vallehermoso.

Optional Extension to Cruz de Tierno

This link is 1.5km (1 mile) long and climbs 165m (540ft). The PR LG 7.1 runs between overgrown terraces and turns right up stone steps to reach a road-end at **El Tión**. Follow the road uphill and keep right at a fork, climbing further up the bendy road to keep right at another junction, reaching a complex road intersection. Turn left for the PR LG 7.1 to reach the Mirador de Roque Blanco and a map-board. The **Restaurante Roque Blanco** lies ahead; otherwise follow the road onwards and gently uphill. It descends slightly at **Cruz de Tierno**, to join the GR 132 (see Walk 23).

WALK 15

Tamargada and Vallehermoso

Distance	7km (4½ miles)
Start	Simancas
Finish	Vallehermoso
Total Ascent	290m (950ft)
Total Descent	620m (2035ft)
Time	2hrs
Terrain	Good roads and tracks, but some paths are a little steep, stony or overgrown.
Refreshment	Plenty of choice in Vallehermoso.
Transport	Buses serve Vallehermoso from San Sebastián and Hermigua, offering access to Simancas.

The PR LG 6 was once a fine circular walk, until part of it was ripped off a hillside during a storm, and another part became badly overgrown. Half the route remains in good condition and allows a short village to village walk from Simancas to Vallehermoso through the Tamargada area.

Route uses PR LG 6 and GR 131.

Start above **Simancas**, where there is a bus shelter at a road junction. Follow the road down through the village to an electricity transformer tower. A concrete road winds further downhill, and on one of the last bends a concrete path is

marked down to the left. Follow this to cross a streambed, then climb as flashed yellow/white. A prominent water pipe runs alongside and the path passes palms and terraces, with good views down the valley. Turn a corner and follow the path down into another valley where there are huddles of houses. Pass palms, prickly pears, aloes, tabaibal, verode and junipers. Go down to a junction and turn right down a steep, stone-paved, well-vegetated path to reach a chapel and plaza at **Pie de la Cuesta**.

Looking down the barranco shortly after leaving Simancas, on the way to Pie de la Cuesta

Walk to the far end of the plaza to join a road. Turn right down the road and left at a junction. Walk down to the right, passing below a house, following a path among palms across a valley. The path has street lights and crosses a streambed before climbing towards houses. Turn left before the first house, up a stone-paved and concrete path to a road-end. Walk up the road to a bend and signpost. Follow a path uphill from the bend, stone-paved at first, pushing past junipers and bushy scrub later, zigzagging up to a gap where there is a view down the barranco, and ahead to Roque Cano.

Looking down the Barranco de la Culata, before joining the GR 131 to Vallehermoso

Looking down the Barranco de la Culata, before joining the GR 131 to Vallehermoso

Go down a steep, stone-paved, stone-strewn zig-zag path, still pushing past junipers and bushy scrub. Keep right twice at junctions with other paths. Descend gradually, passing palms and aloes, then climb a little to pass well above a little reservoir. Descend more steeply and cross the Barranco de la Culata. The path runs level beside an old water channel then winds down past junipers to reach a junction.

Turn left to follow the GR 131 for Vallehermoso. The narrow path crosses steep slopes of tabaibal, tamarisk, juniper, cornical, lavender and aloes. Most of the time there is a water pipe alongside, between cultivated terraces. Look for combined red/yellow/white markers on rocks, walls and pipes, and cross a streambed. Walk up a narrow, well-vegetated path and turn right up a short, stone-paved path to reach a road. Turn left up the road and left again to pass a little bus station on the way to the plaza in the centre of **Vallehermoso**.

WALK 16
Hermigua and Agulo

Distance	9km (5½ miles)
Start	Ibo Alfaro, Hermigua
Finish	Agulo
Total Ascent	800m (2625ft)
Total Descent	775m (2540ft)
Time	3hrs
Terrain	Steep and rugged paths are used for the ascent and descent, with gentler paths, tracks and roads in-between.
Refreshment	Plenty of choice in Hermigua. Bars at Juego de Bolas and Agulo.
Transport	Buses serve Hermigua and Agulo from San Sebastián and Vallehermoso.

Unlikely as it may seem, a splendid path climbs the cliff face on the northern side of the Hermigua valley. This allows access to the national park visitor centre at Juego de Bolas. Another cliff path drops to Agulo, with an optional extension following the GR 132 back to Hermigua.

Start in **Hermigua** at the turning for El Tabaibal and Ibo Alfaro, signposted as the PR LG 4 for Juego de Bolas. Walk up the road, with canes to the left and bananas to the right. Turn right up a concrete road to short-cut a road bend. Turn right along the road, left at the second house, up a concrete path and climb concrete steps above the hotel at **Ibo Alfaro**. Climb to find more concrete steps and yellow/white flashes, eventually reaching a road.

Turn right along the road and pass La Borracha. Climb more steps and keep right of a Casa Rural up a rugged path with log steps. The path winds up a slope of aloes and prickly pears, dotted with palms. There are

Route uses PR LG 4, PR LG 5 and GR 132.

*The route can be
extended round
the coast into the
Hermigua valley to
finish*

steeply-pitched stone steps later, as well as bare rock,
broken fencing and lengths of rope. The scrub becomes
more luxuriant as height is gained. There is a short, level
stretch, even a slight dip, before steps climb to the clifftop. Log steps climb a slope of worn earth as the path
crosses a crest at 700m (2295ft), where heather becomes
quite dense. Walk down to a track and signpost.

Follow the track ahead up to a bend and an intersection. Walk up a narrow path through dense heather
on a worn, brambly groove. Go down past old terraces
to reach a concrete path. Turn right down steps, winding
down to a house and a road. Turn right along the road
through a valley, and turn left over a little bridge. Follow
the road as it winds uphill, then climb a steep and wind-

See Walk 23.

ing path to reach a road junction at **Juego de Bolas**. ◄

Follow the road between the **visitor centre** and Bar
El Tambor, and later fork left up a track cut through red
earth. Wind down past heather trees and cross a scrubby
slope, then head up beside a stand of pines. Reach a fork
in the track in an area of worn red earth and scrubby laurisilva. The GR 132 heads slightly left for Agulo (see Walk

23), while the PR LG 5 heads slightly right, also for Agulo. Keep right and follow the only route passable for vehicles, winding gently downhill with more red earth and less vegetation. Watch for the route swinging right uphill, then left down to a stone-paved **mirador**. There are stunning views of Agulo, in a cultivated hollow surrounded by cliffs.

Follow a road away from the mirador, round a bend, reaching a junction on another bend. Walk down the road for Las Casas del Chorro, turning left to pass above the buildings. Follow the road towards a **reservoir**, Presa de la Palmita, and turn left up a broad path for the Camino de Los Pasos. The path climbs gradually with a wall alongside then descends gradually, becoming steep and rugged. Slopes are covered in prickly pears, tabaibal and incienso. A red earth path leads to a path across a cliff face overlooking Agulo.

Steep zigzags drop down stone steps and rock-steps, needing care all the way down. Cliffs give way to a steep, scrubby slope, where the path features steep, stone-paved zigzags. Continue straight down between walls and terraces to a road. Cross the road and go down steps and a stone-paved path past a builder's yard. Cross a stone-paved road to go down more steps and another stone-paved path, then turn left down a path with railings. Reach a road bend at a signpost, beside a shop and *farmacia* in **Agulo**. Walk down a broad pavement, passing a post office and café to reach a bus shelter.

To extend the walk and return to Hermigua, adding 6.5km (4 miles) to the day's walk, turn left as signposted 'casco urbano'. Follow a level, stone-paved road past a restaurant and a bank, heading gradually down to the Supermercado Gama at a road junction, where the GR 132 passes. Refer to Walk 23 for the route description.

WALK 17

Alto de Garajonay to Hermigua

Distance	13.5 or 20km (8½ or 12½ miles)
Start	Pajaritos, Alto de Garajonay
Finish	Museo Ethnográfico, Hermigua
Total Ascent	150 or 350m (490 or 1150ft)
Total Descent	1350 or 1550m (4430 or 5085ft)
Time	5hrs or 6hrs 30min
Terrain	Good paths down through laurisilva, then a choice of onward routes. Either descend steeply and directly, or stay on gentle paths and tracks in forest, then make a steep descent.
Refreshment	Bar at El Cedro. Plenty of choice in Hermigua.
Transport	Buses serve Pajaritos, near Alto de Garajonay, from San Sebastián and Valle Gran Rey. Buses serve Hermigua from San Sebastián and Vallehermoso.

This route starts on the highest point on La Gomera, Alto de Garajonay, and ends deep in the Hermigua valley. It runs downhill almost all the way, taking in dense laurisilva and some very steep paths towards the end. The route splits on the descent, offering two ways to finish.

Start at a road junction at **Pajaritos** and follow a track signposted for Alto de Garajonay. Turn right up a path with log steps, over a forested hump to cross a dip. Climb more log steps to reach a path junction. Turn left along an easy crest flanked by heather. Drop down log steps to a gap where paths cross, and climb log steps to follow the path to **Alto de Garajonay**, at 1485m (4872ft). ▶ Return back down and up the log steps, along the crest, keeping left for Contadero. Look out for a couple of little miradores on the right. The path is rugged as it winds down log steps to a track. Follow the track downhill, which becomes stone-paved as it reaches a road at **Contadero**.

Route uses PR LG 3 and PR LG 3.1.

See Walk 8 for notes about the summit.

Shafts of light break into the laurisilva forest between Contadero and El Cedro

Cross the road to find the PR LG 3 signposted for El Cedro. The path starts level then winds down log steps marked as a nature trail. The dense laurisilva contains trees of great girth, supporting masses of moss and lichen. Drop to a streambed then climb gradually from it. A gentle descent features a mirador on the left. Log steps and a winding path lead down to another mirador, overlooking a stream. Continue easily to a junction and keep right to follow a path to a river and boulder ford. Cross over and head downstream, later crossing a footbridge and keeping straight ahead at a junction. Walk

▲
Alto de Garajona
1485m

downstream to reach a bend on a track at **Las Mimbreras**.

Turn right to cross the river then turn left down a path for El Cedro. Go down log steps and cross a footbridge then follow the river downstream. Rise gently then go down more log steps and cross another footbridge. Walk up to the **Ermita de Lourdes** and head down to the left for El Cedro. The path is broad and the trees are tall, but then the path narrows and clings to a steep slope. Turn a corner to pass a 'limite del parque' notice and leave the forest. Pass a couple of

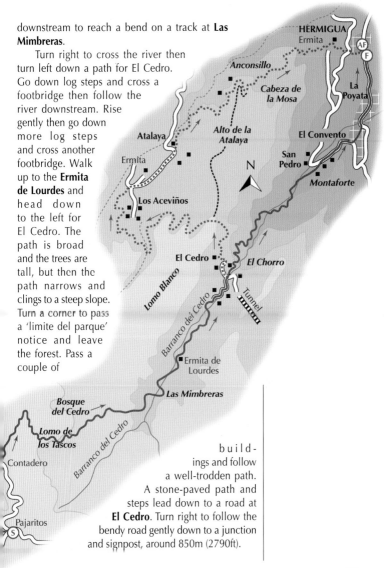

buildings and follow a well-trodden path. A stone-paved path and steps lead down to a road at **El Cedro**. Turn right to follow the bendy road gently down to a junction and signpost, around 850m (2790ft).

Either turn left to follow the PR LG 3.1 (see later) or turn right for the PR LG 3 to Hermigua. After turning right, turn left at another junction to walk down to a house, then go down to a gate. Keep left of the gate and a house, walk downhill and turn right beside a stream, passing below a campsite below the Bar Restaurante La Vista. A stone-paved path passes a pylon then steps lead down into the Hermigua valley. The steps are big and chunky, pitched quite steeply, and need care as they zig-zag through mixed woodland.

The path levels out briefly on a terrace and again beside a reservoir, Presa de los Tilos. Go down steep steps, cross the valley below the dam, and continue across a cliff face with a water pipe alongside. Zigzag down past palms on a slope of lush vegetation, cross a footbridge and continue down the path, crossing a stone footbridge later. Steep stone steps later zigzag down to a small concrete reservoir. Cross a metal footbridge and follow the path onwards. Eventually, the path and pipes level out on a narrow terrace between bananas. Turn

A distinctive blade-like tower of rock is seen most of the way down to San Pedro

right down steep and rugged steps, cross a river and walk downstream on a boulder-paved path among cane thickets. A concrete path reaches a bridge over the river, leading onto a road at **San Pedro**.

Turn right to walk down the road, passing beneath a rock tower that has been prominent throughout the descent. The road runs gently down round a corner, then rises slightly. Turn left on a bend, flashed yellow/white at a concrete seat. Stone steps squeeze between houses to reach the main road in the valley. Turn left to follow it downhill, crossing a bridge to pass the Molino de Gofio Museo. The walk could be finished anywhere in Hermigua, such as beside the Museo Ethnográfico. ▸

The PR LG 3 is signposted across the valley, linking with the GR 132 at a cemetery.

Alternative Route to Hermigua

The PR LG 3.1 is longer and involves more climbing than the PR LG 3. Leave the road junction at **El Cedro** and follow the road down and up to a map-board above the Bar Restaurante La Vista. Follow a path along a terrace above and behind the board, and walk straight along a narrow path, winding uphill and patched with concrete in places. Climb towards El Refugio, keeping below its fragrant garden. Climb to a road junction, cross over and climb a red earth track.

Follow the track across terraces, but watch for a worn groove on the right, climbing into forest. Follow this gradually up and across a crumbling brambly slope. Climb a winding, rocky path, then a groove up a slope of tall laurisilva. An easy, undulating path reaches a track, but just before, turn left to climb up a steep path, passing a 'parque nacional' sign to reach a bend on a higher track. Turn right to walk down to a junction and keep left along another track, heading gently down into a forested valley. The track runs in and out of a series of valleys, rising and falling, generally around 1000m (3280ft). A couple of short-cuts drop to the right for Los Aceviños, then a track junction is reached where the PR LG 3.1 turns right. The track is well-wooded to a 'limite del parque' notice, then more open down to a complex junction at **Los Aceviños**.

Pass a map-board and walk straight down a road, as flashed yellow/white. Pass a few houses and citrus trees, then laurisilva and palms flank the road. At a pronounced left bend, keep straight ahead up a concrete road to a building. Step off the end of the road and go down a narrow forest path to reach a lower concrete road at **Atalya**. Turn right to follow it across the flank of a wooded valley, passing laurisilva, chestnuts and tagasaste. Avoid any turnings to houses while following an undulating track onwards.

A prominent corner is reached around 820m (2690ft), where one track climbs right and another descends left. Take the left one, but walk down a broad path with steps. Turn left down a track, gently at first, then steep and stony. A small mirador offers a splendid view, then the track becomes a steep, stone-paved path with steps, while some parts are stone-strewn. There is a fenced stretch, and a fenced mirador at **Ancosillo**. Further down, pass a ruined caseta with prickly pears. An easy terrace path gives way to zigzags. Go straight down steep stone steps between terraces, passing another caseta. Another level path is followed by more stone steps, then turn a corner and zigzag down to a signpost near a road-end, below the **Ermita de San Juan**.

A steep, stone-paved, zigzag path runs down a slope of lush scrub featuring aloes, prickly pears, tabaibal and cornical, dotted with palms. Pass houses and go down lots of concrete steps to a road. Cross over and go down more winding concrete steps, which give way to rugged stone steps and a steep stone-paved path. A few more steps lead down from a house to a road. Turn right, and almost immediately left, to find a final flight of steep and convoluted concrete steps down to the main road. Turn right to reach the Museo Etnográfico in **Hermigua**.

WALK 18

Santa Catalina and La Caleta

Distance	11km (7 miles)
Start/Finish	Santa Catalina, Hermigua
Total Ascent/Descent	600m (1970ft)
Time	4hrs
Terrain	Good tracks alternate with steep, narrow, stony paths.
Refreshment	Bar at Santa Catalina. Bar off-route at La Caleta.
Transport	Buses serve Hermigua from San Sebastián and Vallehermoso, running close to Santa Catalina.

This convoluted walk starts at Santa Catalina and crosses intricate barrancos around El Moralito and El Palmar. It runs close to La Caleta, where a spur path can be followed to Punta de San Lorenzo, and where a popular little bar can be reached by making a short detour.

If arriving by bus, walk down the road signposted from Hermigua to La Playa, turning right at a junction at **Santa Catalina**. Follow the road between houses and bananas, crossing a bridge over a river to reach a road junction and map-board. The PR LG 2 climbs steps to a lamp post. Turn left up a gritty path, climbing above a couple of ruins on scrubby slopes of tabaibal and verode. Reach a junction between a tarmac road and a dirt road, over 200m (655ft) Turn right up the dirt road as signposted for El

Route uses PR LG 2.

Climbing past a palm tree from the barranco above El Moralito

Moralito and El Palmar. Climb gently, passing a gap offering a view of the Hermigua. Later, reach a bend around a valley where a path is signposted back to Hermigua.

Stay on the dirt road and follow it round to a junction, turning left down a track to **El Moralito**. Keep right of a house, cross a footbridge over the **Barranco de Montoro**, and keep right of another house. Follow steps and a path uphill, walking level into a valley and climbing past a palm tree. Zigzag up a scrubby slope to reach a signpost, turn right and return to the dirt road, over 300m (985ft). Turn left to follow it gently downhill, and turn left again at a junction.

Walk down a track past a valley full of palms, passing a ruined building to reach a white house at **El Palmar**. Turn left and pick a way down between boulders on a scrubby slope to reach a signpost beside a farm. Walk a short way down a track and follow a fence downhill. A path runs between boulders and tabaibal, later crossing a footbridge over a stream in the **Barranco la Barraca**. Climb to a junction and walk straight ahead across a rocky slope on a buttressed path, turning a corner to cross a slope of aloes. Walk gently down to a junction. ▶ Keep left and the path is fenced as it runs gently down and up, then down to a mirador overlooking La Caleta. The path drifts well inland, crossing the **Barranco de Montoro** before climbing to a road. Either turn right down the road to **La Caleta** and the little Macondo bar, or turn left up the road to continue. Walk up the road until the final sweeping bend, which can be cut short using steps on the left, reaching the junction of the tarmac and dirt road passed earlier in the day. All that remains is to walk back down the gritty path and retrace steps to **Santa Catalina** and **Hermigua**. ▶

A right turn leads to the coast at Las Salinas, but if followed, steps must be retraced.

Note that the dirt road links this route with Walk 1. It is easy, but very long and convoluted.

Looking down on La Caleta, where there is a small bar

WALK 19

GR 132: San Sebastián to Playa de Santiago

Distance	22km (13½ miles)
Start	San Sebastián
Finish	Playa de Santiago
Total Ascent/Descent	1050m (3445ft)
Time	7hrs 30min
Terrain	Many good paths across old terraces, but also many steep, stony and rocky paths across rugged barrancos.
Refreshment	Plenty of choice in Playa de Santiago.
Transport	Buses link San Sebastián and Playa de Santiago.

This is one of the longest and driest stages of the GR 132. Walkers need to be self-sufficient, though water is available at a private hotel at El Cabrito. Most of the slopes were terraced long ago, later abandoned to revert to scrub, while farmhouses have crumbled and collapsed.

Leave the bus station in **San Sebastián** to find a map-board across the road. Cross a bridge over a river and walk straight ahead up a road, but veer left down past an ermita. Keep right of a power station, turning left to follow a rugged path climbing beside its boundary fence on a slope of tabaibal and aulaga. Swing gradually right up an easier path overlooking the harbour.

Pass a circular *era*, or threshing floor, then another one beside a ruin. Swing right to walk down into a barranco, crossing its rocky bed and climbing as flashed red/white. The path swings right as it levels, taking in a fine view at a corner where there is a sign for the Monumento Natural Barranco del Cabrito. A rugged path descends, drifting inland to cross the bed of a barranco. Head back towards the coast, passing a white house near **Playa de La Guancha**.

Walking down to Playa de La Guancha, with the Barranco de La Guancha beyond

Head inland past tamarisk along the floor of **Barranco de La Guancha**.

Map continues on page 104

Cross the bouldery bed and follow a path up a scrubby slope, becoming rocky with stone-paved zigzags. Reach a gap, swinging left to climb a little before descending into **Barranco del Cabrito**. Zigzag down to the riverbed, and the path passes a metal bar, crosses a wall and follows a track to reach **Playa del Cabrito**. Turn right along a coastal track to pass a private hotel and reach a map-board. Water is available, but no other facilities.

Turn right along a walled track where a canopy catches rock-fall. Fork left up a path between walls and turn left before a building. The broad, stone-paved path becomes rugged as it zigzags up a steep slope of tabaibal, prickly pears and aloes. Leave the Monumento Natural Barranco del Cabrito at the top and follow the path gently across red pumice and crusty white rock. Cross a hump of bare rock and climb towards the head of a scrubby valley. Walk gently up a path on old terraces, passing tabaibal and verode on the way up towards ruins at **Morales**. Pass below the first houses and between the next, reaching a signpost where the GR 132 joins the PR LG 18.1, around 520m (1705ft).

Turn left as signposted for Playa de Santiago, down a rocky path to cross a barranco, then up across a slight

gap. Go down to cross another barranco then up across a terraced slope. The path drifts down to a rock wall, which is climbed using a breach; then a gentle descent crosses a terraced slope. A rugged path drops into a barranco and climbs up the other side past a ruin. Watch carefully at a corner, turning right to drop into a deeper barranco. Climb the other side to a ruined mansion at **Casas de Contreras**, at 400m (1310ft).

Looking up through the Barranco del Cabrito towards the central mountains of La Gomera

Turn left for the GR 132, passing a couple of tall palms and ruined casetas, then swing right to cross a barranco as marked. Walk along the other side, down past more ruins and across old terraces, passing a ruin near a rocky corner. Follow the path across and gently down terraces then make a sudden right turn down a steep, rugged, zigzag path into **Barranco Chinguarime**. Turn left down the bouldery bed, then right to reach bananas. Walk past a signpost and turn left up a dirt road, but watch for steps and a zigzag path climbing right. A level terrace path near the top leads to a house at El Joradillo.

Keep left of the house to follow a road, but leave it as signposted down a zigzag path flanked by low walls.

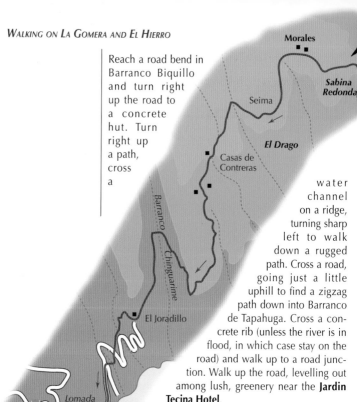

Reach a road bend in Barranco Biquillo and turn right up the road to a concrete hut. Turn right up a path, cross a water channel on a ridge, turning sharp left to walk down a rugged path. Cross a road, going just a little uphill to find a zigzag path down into Barranco de Tapahuga. Cross a concrete rib (unless the river is in flood, in which case stay on the road) and walk up to a road junction. Walk up the road, levelling out among lush, greenery near the **Jardin Tecina Hotel**.

Reach a road junction near a supermarket and restaurant, where taxis are available. Turn left down the road overlooking Playa de Santiago. Go down stone steps on the left to reach a couple of shops and a bus shelter at **Laguna de Santiago**. Walk straight along the road, through a banana plantation, onto the Promenade Avenida Maritima through **Playa de Santiago**. Apartments, pensión, banks with ATMs, post office, shops, bars, restaurants, buses and taxis. Tourist information office, tel. 922-895650.

WALK 20
GR 132: Playa de Santiago to La Dama

Distance	18km (11 miles)
Start	Playa de Santiago
Finish	La Dama
Total Ascent	1320m (4330ft)
Total Descent	1100m (3610ft)
Time	6hrs
Terrain	A long and gradual ascent, followed by a series of barranco crossings where paths are sometimes steep and rugged.
Refreshment	Bars at Alajeró and La Dama.
Transport	Buses link Playa de Santiago with San Sebastián, Alajeró and Valle Gran Rey. Buses also link La Dama, Chipude and Vallehermoso.

This stage of the GR 132 starts with a long climb to Alajeró, followed by a series of deep, steep, rugged barrancos. Small farms and the remote village of Arguayoda are passed, then an enormous barranco has to be crossed at La Rajita to reach La Dama.

Start on the Plaza El Carmen in **Playa de Santiago**. There is a stage on the plaza and a barranco behind it. Follow a road inland, passing the Centro de Salud (Health Centre). Cross a footbridge and continue upstream, turning left up a tarmac road with a railing. Zigzag up concrete steps, walk up a tiled path, and turn right up more concrete steps, reaching a building with communication masts. Turn right up past more buildings to reach a road bend at **Las Trincheras**.

Turn right on the road, then almost immediately left. A rugged path climbs a scrubby slope past a few more houses. Pipes run beside the path and the scrub includes tabaibal, verode and cornical. A tall fence leads back to the road. Turn right to walk up the road and pass the airport access. Café, buses and taxis. Follow the main road until a path is signposted up to the right, accompanied by a pipeline, beside a deep barranco. Keep right of two small farmhouses, climb to a signpost and keep right up a narrow road. Pass a concrete dam and climb past a house on old terraces. The path continues beside the pipeline to **Antoncojo**.

Turn left up a narrow road and climb steps to a bend on the main road, to a map-board and bus shelter. Turn right, then immediately right again as signposted for Antoncojo, then left as signposted for Alajeró. The path and pipeline lead up a slope of rugged terraces but keep left of a house. Pass near a road bend and follow the path and pipeline up beside a fence. Turn round a bend on the main road then follow the path and pipeline uphill again. Cross the road and walk up a concrete road. Don't go left to a house, but walk straight up a concrete, stone-paved path, passing aloes and palms. Walk up another road and turn left at the top into **Alajeró**. Hotel, bars, post office, ATM and buses.

Walk ahead as signposted for the 'centro urbano' while palms and prickly pears flank the road. Rise gradually past a couple of bars and the Molino de Gofio. Turn left at the church, through the Plaza de la Iglesia, passing a big tree and turning right up concrete steps. A signpost points down a road for La Dama. Walk gently up and down the road, around 840m (2755ft).

At the end of the road a stone-paved path zigzags down a steep slope of cistus and prickly pears. Pass a little reservoir then climb towards palms. There is a glimpse of a farm at **Magaña**, but keep straight ahead down a rough, boulder-paved path, down a ridge overlooking the **Barranco de Charco Hondo**. Reach palms and a house, keeping right to join a road. Turn left down the road, with barrancos on both sides while passing a gap. Walk along the undulating road to the end of the tarmac, turning right down a dirt road. A rocky path passes a house and a rugged path runs along the edge of a barranco to a palm tree.

Walk down a path across a steep slope of tabaibal, prickly pears and cistus, hacked from red pumice, narrow at times, with stone-paved zigzags past rocky outcrops and cliffs to reach palms in the **Barranco de La Negra**. Cross a stream and continue gently, level at times, passing above ruins at **La Negra**. Turn right to walk into the next barranco and cross its bed among palms. Walk up the path and be sure to turn right up stone-paved zigzags. The path is fenced on both sides as it reaches buildings at **La Manteca**.

Do not go through a gate in a fence as a signpost might suggest, but turn left just above, watching for red/white flashes. A nasty stretch of path picks a way across a rugged, overgrown, weak layer between cliffs, running round and down into a little barranco. A good stone-paved path climbs, turning right at the top. A level path crosses

Map continues on page 108

toncojo

Airport

Las Trincheras

PLAYA DE SANTIAGO

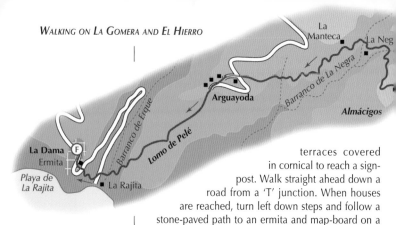

terraces covered in cornical to reach a signpost. Walk straight ahead down a road from a 'T' junction. When houses are reached, turn left down steps and follow a stone-paved path to an ermita and map-board on a tiny plaza in **Arguayoda**.

Follow a paved road over a hump and turn left down a rugged path. Cross a road to reach a track and turn right to follow the track downhill. There is a long and gradual descent, then a bendy stretch. Watch for a signpost on the right and go down a zigzag path on a steep, rocky slope. When an electricity transformer tower is reached, cross the bouldery **Barranco de Erque** and look for a way up

The view back down to La Rajita from the path climbing to La Dama

through tamarisk bushes. Turn left down a road to reach a ruin on the right at **La Rajita**. ▶ Climb steps to find a rugged zigzag path up a steep and rocky slope. At the top turn left along a road, then right up steps to short-cut to a church at **La Dama**. Walk up the road to a map-board, bus shelter and bars. The village is noted for its banana plantations, but offers no accommodation.

The buildings were part of a self-contained settlement around a fish processing plant.

La Dama is noted for its extensive banana plantations

WALK 21

GR 132: La Dama to Arure

Distance	23km (14¼ miles)
Start	La Dama
Finish	Mirador del Santo, Arure
Total Ascent	1570m (5150ft)
Total Descent	1090m (3575ft)
Time	8hrs
Terrain	Good tracks and paths most of the way, but some are steep and rugged on the way in and out of barrancos.
Refreshment	Bars at La Dama, Valle Gran Rey and Arure.
Transport	Buses link Valle Gran Rey and Arure with Chipude, Alajeró, Playa de Santiago and San Sebastián.

This stage starts with a succession of little barrancos and a long climb to the Barranco de Argaga. There is an option to scramble down through the rugged barranco. The route could be split at Valle Gran Rey, though for the sake of one steep climb, an easy high-level path leads to Arure.

Follow the road uphill to leave La Dama, passing a banana crop. A signpost on the left indicates the GR 132 for Valle Gran Rey. Follow a track gently across a slope of grass and tabaibal, making a lazy zigzag to cross Barranco Samarardón. Climb gently and turn sharp right across a ridge. Head downhill and, before reaching terraces of bananas, turn left to follow the track further down. At the next sharp bend switch to a path across a steep, scrubby, rocky slope. Drop down at the end to cross the bouldery bed of the barranco and head for Playa de Iguala.

Follow a zigzag path climbing to the top of Punta de Iguala. Turn right and walk up a rugged, stony slope. Keep left of the crumbling walls of old terraces at **El Verodal**, turning right and left above them. Walk up to a couple of buildings and keep right of them. A winding access track could be followed up Loma de Gerián, but watch for red/white flashes indicating a path following an old water channel along the edge of a barranco. Pass old terraces and keep climbing, level out for a while then climb again. Walk along and up a track, reaching a junction with a road.

Turn left as signposted for Valle Gran Rey. Either follow the bendy road, or turn right to short-cut up a dead straight old water channel. If following the channel, when the road is reached for the third time, turn left to walk down to a bend. If following the road, watch for the bend and keep straight ahead, more or less following a pylon line. A narrow path flanked by low stone walls climbs to houses on the skyline at **Gerián**. Reach the nearest building and cross a road between it and some palms. Climb to the right to follow a wall and fence. Join a road and walk up to a signpost. ▶

Walk up the road to stay on the GR 132, but take the first path left, along the edge of the barranco, then take the first path right. Climb to a road bend, but head left to follow a concrete water channel a short way. Switch to a boulder-paved path up to a road and turn left down it to the **Ermita de Guadalupe**. Walk down a

Walk 6 drops into the **Barranco de Argaga**, offering an alternative route.

Map continues on page 113

111

A walker climbs the path that the GR 132 follows down into Valle Gran Rey

few steps to pick up and follow the water channel again, reaching a junction where the PR I G 13.2 arrives from Chipude (see Walk 7).

Turn left down past aloes, prickly pears and palms to reach the rocky bed of the barranco. Cross over and climb, then follow a level terrace. A gentle climb leads to the rocky gap of **Degollada de los Bueyes**. Follow an obvious path winding downhill; some parts are level, other parts drop steeply and some short stretches climb. Wind between cliffs and rocky outcrops, with splendid views of Valle Gran Rey. Reach a house among palms at the bottom and turn left. Walk down a rugged, boulder-paved path, along an easier terrace path, leaving the Parque Rural Valle Gran Rey. Head down to follow a path with railings and turn left to reach the **Ermita de Los Reyes** and its plaza.

Walk down steps into the barranco to cross its bouldery bed and a track. Follow a stone-paved path through thickets of cane and climb stone steps with railings to reach the main road at **El Guro**. Use a pedestrian crossing and turn left down the road. Bar, shop and buses. The pavement expires and there is a roadside parking strip. Climb stone steps on the right, passing houses to follow a path hacked from rock. Walk down steps to a road and turn right to follow it gently uphill, parallel to the main road. Keep right at the Centro de Salud, passing apartments and turning round a bend to find a signpost at **La Calera**. Shops, bars, buses and taxis.

Turn right up steps signposted for Arure and turn left across a streambed to follow a stone-paved path and steps. Zigzag up past a notice for the Parque Rural Valle Gran Rey. Aloes and prickly pears give way to tamarisk, tabaibal, verode, cornical and aromatic shrubs, dominated by lavender. Keep climbing, looking up to see how columnar cliffs seem to support a peak. This is an illusion and afterwards the slope is less severe and rocky. Look for a couple of telegraph poles as the gradient eases considerably, giving way to a gentle, stony, gravelly, dusty path up old terraces where tabaibal and cornical grow.

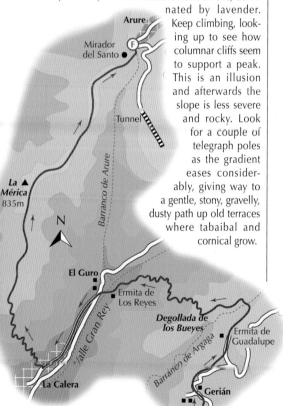

113

Looking down to the west coast of La Gomera from a track near Arure

A ruined house stands to the left while an era stands to the right. The path is broad and stony, with a big stone step every few paces. Pass a ruin and a limekiln and continue up a boulder-paved path on scrubby terraces. The broad, undulating path has been hacked from a cliff, passing a cave, then drops and climbs past pines on a steep slope of crumbling red pumice. Cross a little gap for a view down to the coast, and later cross another gap. A steep, stone-paved path drops to a track. Turn left, in effect straight ahead, rising with views on both sides of the crest to reach a goat farm. Descend to join a road and climb past a few houses to a map-board. The GR 132 turns left, but to visit **Arure** follow the road straight ahead. Bars, shops and buses.

WALK 22

GR 132: Arure to Vallehermoso

Distance	15km (9½ miles)
Start	Mirador del Santo, Arure
Finish	Vallehermoso
Total Ascent	630m (2065ft)
Total Descent	1250m (4100ft)
Time	6hrs
Terrain	Mostly rugged paths with steep stretches and varied vegetation. Some easy stretches along roads and tracks.
Refreshment	Bars at Alojera and Chorros de Epina. Plenty of choice in Vallehermoso.
Transport	Buses link Alojera and Chorros de Epina with Vallehermoso. Buses also link Chorros de Epina, Vallehermoso, Chipude and La Dama.

This stage starts with an exciting cliff-face traverse in the Monumento Natural Lomo del Carretón. The route drops to Alojera then climbs to the fringe of laurisilva forest at Chorros de Epina. A long and winding ridge descends to Vallehermoso, couched in a deep and verdant valley.

Walk from **Arure**, down the main road to a bend, where a signpost points right for the Mirador del Santo. Follow the road to a map-board, turn right up a stone-paved path and pass through an arch. Enjoy views from the **Mirador del Santo** then walk past an ermita to follow the Camino de las Correderas, across a steep slope of pines. The path exploits a soft, red layer between harder rocks, climbing gently then descending past palms. Scrubby slopes and stone steps zigzag to a lower terrace, where the path undulates past tabaibal and cistus. Walk beneath sheer cliffs, passing prickly pears to reach palms. The path winds in and out of buttresses and gullies then descends.

Looking over the edge from the Camino de las Correderas on Lomo del Carretón

Tight zigzags drop down past pines and longer zigzags run down a scrubby slope. The path becomes a stony groove, past aloes and palms to a pylon, continuing past junipers and scrub to a road bend. Cross over and walk further down, crossing a couple of streambeds among palms. Climb gradually to houses and an electricity transformer tower. Turn left down a road into **Alojera**, passing apartments on the way down to a plaza and church, near the Bar Plaza. Turn right and right again, down to a road junction with shady palms, the Centro Social Alojera, bus shelter and map-board.

Follow a bendy road up past a supermarket and Bar Perdomo. Turn left down concrete steps, right at the bottom and almost immediately left. Go past the last house and down a grassy path to cross a streambed. Walk upstream a little and turn left, watching for red/white flashes while climbing a crumbling barranco. Cross it and almost climb to a road, but climb to a track instead which leads up to a road junction.

Cross the road and climb as signposted up

VALLEHERMOSO

Lomo de Los Cochinos

Montaña Blanca

La Quilla

N

Epina

Bar

Ermita
Chorros de Epina

a winding path on a slope of sparse scrub. Avoid a road bend, but step onto the road at a higher bend, among richer scrub. Walk up the road then up a short path between walls. Climb alongside water pipes, passing bushy scrub, with palms and pines at a house. Clip a road bend and walk up a track, still following pipes. A ramp drops to the road and the road is followed uphill a little.

Walk down a stone-paved track, swinging left across terraces of palms, prickly pears, aloes and incienso. The track narrows as it passes ruins. Climb between walls, rugged at first then up a fine stone-paved path with steps, where the vegetation is lush and dense. Cross the road to climb further, the path becoming rugged again. Cross the road and later pass bramble-tangled scrub and palms, then a good path with steps leads up to the road again.

Cross the road one last time and follow the path up a slope of dense scrub. There are grassy slopes further uphill then heather trees. Climb to a concrete water store and the path runs gently among pines. Climb to a junction and fork right. Pines grow on the left and laurisilva on the right. An overgrown stretch of path leads to a signpost, followed by the Ermita de San Isidro at **Chorros de Epina**. Turn left down stone steps to have a look at a curious spring on the left (see Walk 11). Double back past the steps to follow the path signposted for Vallehermoso, up a wooded slope to a road around 800m (2625ft). Turn left to reach the Restaurante Los Chorros de Epina.

Follow the main road down through a cutting and turn left along the road for Alojera. Enjoy fine views then turn right up a narrow road. Pass below a prominent communications mast on **Montaña Blanca**. Turn right as signposted down a bendy track, where eucalyptus grows among laurisilva. Turn right again down a path, where palms grow among laurisilva. The path makes a falling traverse, then a steep groove runs down through laurisilva, passing prickly pears. ◄ Laurisilva gives way to junipers and prickly pears, and the path occasionally runs level along the crest, or winds downhill rugged and stone-paved, with one narrow and awkward stretch.

*There are good views as the path switches sides along the crest of **Lomo de Los Cochinos**.*

There is a view of Vallehermoso from a slope of junipers, and the path crosses the crest for a view down to Playa de Vallehermoso. It crosses back round a crest of aloes to reach a house. Go down winding concrete steps, passing more houses to reach a road in **Vallehermoso**. Cross the road and go down steps to reach the Bar Cafeteria Chamire. Turn right into the plaza in the centre of town.

Walking down Lomo de Los Cochinos towards Vallehermoso

WALK 23

GR 132: Vallehermoso to Hermigua

Distance	19km (12 miles)
Start	Vallehermoso
Finish	Las Nuevitas, Hermigua
Total Ascent	1000m (3280ft)
Total Descent	1100m (3610ft)
Time	7hrs
Terrain	A steep climb, then gentler forest and farmland. A rugged descent to the coast, then road-walking.
Refreshment	Bars at Juego de Bolas, Agulo, Santa Catalina and Hermigua.
Transport	Buses link Vallehermoso, Agulo and Hermigua with San Sebastián.

This stage climbs from Vallehermoso to pass Roque Cano. The high ground beyond is mostly gentle, passing the national park visitor centre at Juego de Bolas. A steep and rugged descent leads to Agulo and along the coast to the deep and verdant Hermigua valley.

Start in the centre of Vallehermoso, where a four-way signpost shows routes out of the plaza. For the PR LG 7 leave the plaza and walk down the main road, as signposted for Garabato. Turn right, again signposted for Garabato and walk up the road. Keep left at a junction, up round a bend, then turn right up concrete steps. Turn right up a road to reach a junction and signpost. The GR 132 turns left up the road, continuing up a broad, stone-paved path. Keep straight ahead at a junction, zigzagging up a slope dotted with palms, aloes, prickly pears and junipers.

Pass a notice for the Monumento Natural Roque Cano then climb past the monstrous **Roque Cano** itself.

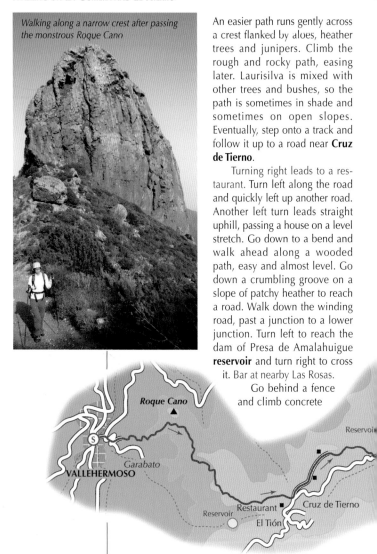

Walking along a narrow crest after passing the monstrous Roque Cano

An easier path runs gently across a crest flanked by aloes, heather trees and junipers. Climb the rough and rocky path, easing later. Laurisilva is mixed with other trees and bushes, so the path is sometimes in shade and sometimes on open slopes. Eventually, step onto a track and follow it up to a road near **Cruz de Tierno**.

Turning right leads to a restaurant. Turn left along the road and quickly left up another road. Another left turn leads straight uphill, passing a house on a level stretch. Go down to a bend and walk ahead along a wooded path, easy and almost level. Go down a crumbling groove on a slope of patchy heather to reach a road. Walk down the winding road, past a junction to a lower junction. Turn left to reach the dam of Presa de Amalahuigue **reservoir** and turn right to cross it. Bar at nearby Las Rosas.

Go behind a fence and climb concrete

steps to a road. Turn right, level out, and climb again to the gates of Finca Mariolga y Manuel. A few concrete steps climb to the left and a stony groove climbs a slope of heather. Keep left of a pylon, levelling out, then rise gently to a red-earth shoulder near two pylons. Pass a marker post and keep level, then later drop beside a low fence. Cross a road-end and go down a worn groove with a few steps, past little buildings. Cross a valley and wind up the other side climbing gently among pines. Cross a road and walk ahead, gently down a track. Turn left along a road and walk to the visitor centre at **Juego de Bolas**.

The national park visitor centre is full of interesting exhibits and offers plenty of information about the natural wonders of La Gomera. It gets busy when tour buses roll in, often carrying day-trippers from Tenerife. Tel. 922-800993.

Follow the road between the visitor centre and Bar El Tambor, and later fork left up a track cut through red earth. Wind down past heather trees and cross a scrubby slope, then rise beside a stand of pines.

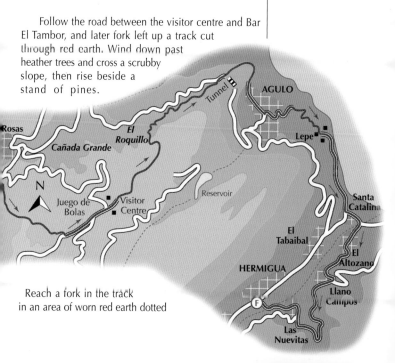

Reach a fork in the track in an area of worn red earth dotted

Following a red earth path after leaving the visitor centre at Juego de Bolas

with scrubby laurisilva. The GR 132 heads slightly left for Agulo, while the PR LG 5 heads slightly right (see Walk 16), also for Agulo. Keep left to go down gentle log steps on a broad path, partly fenced, beside an eroded gully.

The path is stone-paved and cobbled, with lots of zigzags down a well-vegetated slope. Pass a building at La Palmita and continue down, levelling out on red earth, then heading down to a main road. Turn right down the road, cross over, and beware of traffic at the **Túnel de Agulo**. Walk down a concrete ramp near oranges. The path drops steeply past crumbling cliffs to a stone-paved road at a cemetery. Turn right, down and up a road through **Agulo**. Keep left up Calle del Calvario, passing the odd shop and bar. Walk down to the church, then down Calle del Pintor Aguiar.

Reach a stone-paved road junction and walk to the Supermercado Gama, turning left down a tarmac road. Turn right down a steep and winding road, past bananas. Walk down concrete steps at the Balcon del Callao, which become exceptionally steep. Turn right across a terrace then go down more steps into a barranco choked with cane. Follow a path across terraces and climb stone-paved and concrete steps. Turn left along a path between houses, flashed red/white. Turn down to the left, then to the right to reach a little paved plaza at **Lepe**.

Turn left down a narrow tarmac road to Playa de Hermigua, turning right uphill and inland. Turn left down a road between houses and bananas at **Santa Catalina**, crossing a bridge over a river to reach a road junction and map-board. Turn right up a bendy road to pass houses at **El Altozano** and **Llano Campos**. The road turns round a convoluted side-valley to reach houses at **Las Nuevitas**.

The GR 132 continues along the road, but if staying in Hermigua, then detour off-route. Watch for a signpost at a junction for the PR LG 4 to Ibo Alfaro, and follow a bendy road downhill, across the valley, and up to the plaza and church in **Hermigua**.

WALK 24

GR 132: Hermigua to San Sebastián

Distance	19km (12 miles)
Start	Las Nuevitas, Hermigua
Finish	San Sebastián
Total Ascent	750m (2460ft)
Total Descent	850m (2790ft)
Time	6hrs
Terrain	Easy road-walking at the start and finish. Steep winding paths over the highest part.
Refreshment	Plenty of choice in San Sebastián.
Transport	Buses link Hermigua with Vallehermoso and San Sebastián.

The final stage of the GR 132 starts with a convoluted climb from the Hermigua valley to cross the forested Cumbre. A direct descent on the other side is initially rugged, followed by a simple road-walk back to San Sebastián, completing the circuit round La Gomera.

Walkers who stayed in Hermigua must retrace their steps to **Las Nuevitas**. Follow the road onwards, eventually passing a **cemetery**. Continue gently down the road to a junction, turning left for **La Poyata**. At the end of the road, go down winding concrete steps and cross a footbridge over a river. Zigzag up to the main road, turn left round a bend, and go down concrete steps on the left. Follow a path below the road, later walking beside pipes. Don't be tempted to cross a stream, but follow the pipes until a concrete path leads up to a road.

Turn left up the bendy road, crossing a bridge over the stream. Turn left up a steep, narrow road, then turn right past a house and climb grassy log steps, with a view of a nearby **reservoir**, Presa de Mulagua. The path runs gently down to cross a stream among palms, then crosses a couple more side-valleys. Stone steps wind uphill then log steps and a grassy path, sometimes with ropes alongside. Heather trees grow at a higher level, where the path has stone steps and more ropes.

Reach a building on a road at **La Carbonera**. ▸ Cross the road and follow a winding path up a wooded slope, passing a 'parque nacional' sign and a house. A zigzag path climbs further, sometimes in dense laurisilva. Later, contour across a steep slope, reaching a gap, **Degollada de la Cumbre**. This is the highest point on this stage, at 857m (2812ft). Laurisilva gives way to a steep slope of prickly pears and aloes, though during the descent the path winds past cistus and fragrant incienso. There are sharp bends and a brief view of a **farmhouse restaurant** before the path becomes rough and broken, landing on a main road.

Cross the road and turn left to walk parallel, through a little cutting. Either go to the farmhouse restaurant, or turn right as signposted for the GR 132.

There is a nearby road tunnel beneath the Cumbre.

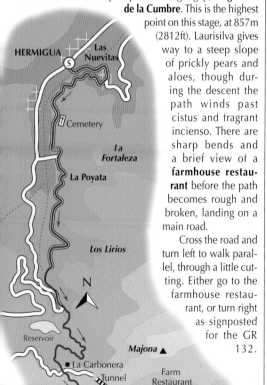

Map continues on page 126

The path is initially good on a slope of grass, aloes and prickly pears, but rugged on the way down a rocky streambed, later crossing the stream. Climb past palms and head downhill past more to reach a road-end at **Aguajilva**. Walk down the bendy road and keep straight ahead at a junction. Masses of cardón grow on rugged slopes nearby, as well as cane thickets in the riverbed. There are houses,

The view back towards the forested Cumbre on the descent to Lomo Fragoso

126

farms and the Bodegón Lomo Fragoso. Turn left to walk down past a pizzería to reach the Bar El Atajo at **Lomo Fragoso**.

Simply walk down the road, all the way through the **Barranco de La Villa** to San Sebastián. It sounds simple, but it is 6.5km (4 miles) to the town centre. Pass **San Antonio** and pass the Bar Restaurante La Cabaña at **El Langrero**. The road turns left to

cross a bridge over the barranco then turns right past an ambulance station. Follow the road into **San Sebastián**, keeping left as signposted 'centro ciudad' under a road bridge. Walk straight into the town centre.

127

WALK 25

GR 132.1: Igualero to La Dama

Distance	11km (7 miles)
Start	Igualero
Finish	La Dama
Total Ascent	420m (1380ft)
Total Descent	1920m (6300ft)
Time	5hrs
Terrain	Paths are sometimes steep, rugged and overgrown on the descent. There are steep climbs in the middle and at the end.
Refreshment	Bars in La Dama.
Transport	Buses serve Igualero from San Sebastián, Playa de Santiago and Valle Gran Rey. Buses link La Dama with Chipude and Vallehermoso.

The GR 132.1 offers a link between the GR 131 and GR 132. It runs from Igualero, high on the slopes of Alto de Garajonay, down the rugged Barranco de Erque to La Dama. The scenery is often spectacular, but the paths are sometimes very rugged.

Start at a bus shelter at **Igualero**, around 1300m (4265ft). Walk down through the village to find a signpost on the left for the GR 131. A path winds down and swings right along a terrace to leave the village, reaching a junction where the GR 132.1 turns sharp left for Erquito, Arguayoda and La Dama. The route is initially along a vague terrace path, dropping into a barranco. Cross over and rise gently, passing beneath a cliff and going round a rocky corner. Walk down to a signpost and turn right downhill.

The path isn't clear through bouldery cistus scrub but follow a crest and watch for cairns. The ground levels out and the descent begins in earnest to the right of a rocky

crest, marked by a cairn. The path runs down a worn, stony, bouldery groove. Watch carefully to stay on it and look down the barranco to see houses linked by a very bendy road. At one point the path turns sharp right and is overgrown with tabaibal and verode. Consider a scramble down to a pylon, regaining the path as it turns left round a corner.

Looking into the Barranco de Erque from the rugged path from Igualero to Erquito

The path is often wet as it contours past an overhang. Zigzag down past prickly pears and aloes, passing a couple of palms. Watch carefully for the path on the final zigzags, though it is also possible to head straight down a slope of crumbling red rock. If doing this, follow small cairns. The path does not go down to the nearest houses, or to the bendy road, but turns left round a corner. Red/white flashes appear and a signpost points left at a junction. Drop down to cross a streambed and rise to reach a road-end at **Erquito**, over 700m (2295ft), where there are houses and almonds.

Turn left uphill as signposted for Arguayoda and La Dama. Pass a notice that mentions the

Map continues on page 130

129

Between 1950 and 1980 the population of La Gomera halved, but 400 people left this area, leaving only two inhabitants.

depopulation of the area. ◄ A steep stone-paved path climbs from the notice, passing almonds, aloes, prickly pears and tabaibal, slicing across crumbling red pumice, passing a signpost. It is paved as it crosses a cliff-face, then zigzags uphill. Keep left as marked at a junction, following a narrower zigzag path, reaching the top around 900m (290ft) on the slopes of **Montaña de La Vega**.

Walk ahead and contour between old terraces, turning right downhill then left to contour again, passing above a ruined caseta. Turn a corner, passing between a couple more ruins, heading down and up while passing between terraces of almonds. The path keeps right, or straight ahead, at a junction, where there are lots of prickly pears. Wind down past small ruins and a substantial ruined house, all surrounded by prickly pears. Land at the junction of a track and a road bend, where there is a signpost. Walk down a rugged slope of tabaibal, following a zigzag path. Watch for the red/white flashed route past houses at **El Drago**.

A stone-paved path with steps leads down to a circular threshing floor, and a narrow tarmac road. Turn right, passing fences,

then turn left down another clear path accompanied by a water pipe down to a road bend. Walk ahead, off the bend, down a narrow road, and

A ruined caseta perched above the barranco on the way down to Arguayoda

pass the last house on the slope. Follow a vague and rugged path, still accompanied by a water pipe on a scrubby slope. The path runs along the edge of the barranco, avoiding a road bend. Walk down past aulaga and aloes on dry terraces. Land on a road and go down steps and a stone-paved path to a tiny ermita and a map-board on a tiny plaza in **Arguayoda**.

Follow a paved road over a hump and turn left down a rugged path. Cross a road to reach a track and turn right to follow the track downhill. There is a long and gradual descent, then a bendy stretch. Watch for a signpost on the right and go down a zigzag path on a steep, rocky slope. When an electricity transformer tower is reached, cross the bouldery **Barranco de Erque** and look for a way up through tamarisk bushes. Turn left down a road to reach a ruin on the right at **La Rajita**. Climb steps to find a rugged zigzag path up a steep and rocky slope. At the top turn left along a road, then right up steps to short-cut to a church at **La Dama**. Walk up the road to a map-board, bus shelter and bars. The village offers no accommodation.

WALK 26

GR 131: Playa de Vallehermoso to Chipude

Distance	17.5km (11 miles)
Start	Playa de Vallehermoso
Finish	Chipude
Total Ascent	1500m (4920ft)
Total Descent	340m (1115ft)
Time	7hrs
Terrain	Mostly easy roads and tracks, but some steep, forested paths.
Refreshment	Plenty of choice in Vallehermoso. Bars at Las Hayas, El Cercado and Chipude.
Transport	Buses serve Vallehermoso from San Sebastián. Buses serve Chipude from Vallehermoso, Valle Gran Rey, Playa de Santiago and San Sebastián.

The GR 131 runs coast-to-coast through La Gomera, starting at Playa de Vallehermoso and finishing in San Sebastián. It can be completed in two days, or split into shorter sections. A long climb from Vallehermoso gives way to easier walking from village to village to Chipude.

Reach **Playa de Vallehermoso** by a short taxi ride from Vallehermoso. Visit the peculiar Castillo del Mar, built for shipping bananas, and the Guanche burial site of Cueva de Las Palomas. A bar restaurant beside a swimming pool is rarely open. A map-board explains about the GR 131 and its connection with the E7 spanning Europe. Follow the road up through the valley to reach a bus shelter. Turn left down a road, across the valley and up past a few houses at **Valle Abajo** to reach the road-end. Follow a path onwards round the side-valley of Barranco de la Culata. Zigzag up to a junction and turn left to follow the GR 131 for Vallehermoso. The narrow path crosses steep slopes of tabaibal, tamarisk, juniper, cornical, lavender, and aloes. Most of the time there is a water pipe alongside, between cultivated terraces. Look for combined red/yellow/white markers on rocks, walls and pipes, and cross a streambed. Walk up a narrow, well-vegetated path and turn right up a short, stone-paved path to reach a road. Turn left up the road and left again to pass a little bus station on the way to the plaza in the centre of **Vallehermoso**.

Map continues on page 134

A four-way signpost shows routes out of the plaza. For the GR 131, pass the post office (Correos), walk up the road and turn right as signposted for El Carmen and Barranco del Ingenio. Fork right almost immediately, up a steep, narrow road signposted for the GR 131. This bendy road climbs past houses, farms and lush terraces of vegetables. Climb until the road curves round on itself at **Los Chapines**, where a track on the right is signposted for the GR 131. Climb through a bushy valley passing palms, cistus, canes, calcosas, heather trees and the occasional juniper. Follow the winding track or watch for steep, narrow paths shortcutting bends. When the track becomes overgrown, a path is signposted on the right.

Follow the path up along a crest, off to one side and down to a narrow gap. Although laurisilva

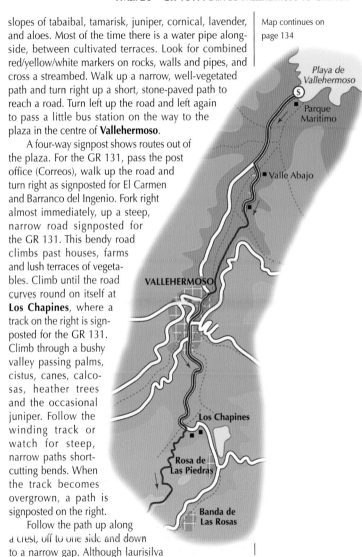

133

tries to assert itself, there are also aloes, prickly pears and palms. Climb a groove through taller laurisilva onto an open hump. Continue uphill or contour across the slopes of Lomo del Corte, passing more prickly pears and a few aloes. Reach a track on a gap at **La Vistita del Rosario**, at 745m (2445ft).

Views are lost as the GR 131 climbs log steps, passing a 'limite del parque' notice. The laurisilva becomes very dense and mossy as log steps lead up to a junction. Turn left as flashed red/white, reaching a road at almost 1100m (3610ft). Turn left and walk gently down the road, crossing over after passing signs for Las Creces and Las Hayas.

Walk gently down a track to reach a small car park at **Las Creces**. Follow the gently undulating, winding track onwards until a sign points left for Las Hayas. A path climbs through tall, dense laurisilva, passing grotesquely bent heather trees to reach the edge of the forest. Turn left up to a 'limite del parque' notice, then head downhill and keep right of an ermita. A rugged track and path run between houses and fences then a short access road runs down to a road bend. Walk down to a crossroads and map-board at **Las Hayas**.

The Bar Restaurante La Montaña is nearby; otherwise, turn left down a road signposted for El Cercado and Chipude. Walk round a valley of terraces and palms then head uphill. Go down through a crossroads and turn left as signposted down a path. When a junction is reached, fork left up a path, passing palms, to reach another junction on a crest. Walk straight ahead across a slope of tagasaste and cistus, and down a boulder-paved

Banda de Las Rosas

La Vistita del Rosario

Los Loros

La Meseta

Araña

Las Creces

Cabeza de la Vizcaína

Las Hayas

El Cercado

College

Chipude

zigzag. A level path passes beneath an overhang, with the barranco falling steeply below. Drop down past terraces, cross a streambed, and contour across a terrace with a view down to Valle Gran Rey. Cross another streambed and climb winding stone steps on a slope of cistus, tagasaste and heather trees. A road bend is reached at the Bar Maria in **El Cercado**.

Turn right to follow the road to the Bar Restaurant Victoria. Further along the road are traditional pottery shops. Go down steps to follow a concrete path below the road, flashed red/white. Turn right down a road, round a bend, and before reaching a signpost, turn left up a broad, stone-paved path. Cross the main road and walk up a broad path. Walk up a slope of cistus and aloes, cross a crest and go down a stone-paved path on terraces bearing palms and aloes. Cross the main road, continue down across the terraced valley and climb up the other side.

Turn right along the main road past a few houses then turn left up steps. The path climbs then runs level and rocky towards a ruin. Turn right, then quickly left up another rugged path. Turn right up concrete steps and follow a concrete path. Turn right down a stone-paved road, then quickly left to a bus shelter and map-board beside the plaza in the middle of **Chipude**, around 1060m (3480ft). Hotel Sonia, shop, bars and buses to most parts of La Gomera.

The paved path that links the villages of El Cercado and Chipude

WALK 27

GR 131: Chipude to San Sebastián

Distance	25km (15½ miles)
Start	Chipude
Finish	San Sebastián
Total Ascent	800m (2625ft)
Total Descent	1960m (6430ft)
Time	8hrs
Terrain	Optional scramble, otherwise rugged paths rise and fall, sometimes on forested slopes, before a long and rugged descent.
Refreshment	Bars at Apartadero and Degollada de la Peraza. Plenty of choice in San Sebastián.
Transport	Buses serve Chipude, Pajaritos and Degollada de Peraza from Valle Gran Rey, Playa de Santiago and San Sebastián.

After the GR 131 leaves Chipude there is an option to climb La Fortaleza, requiring hands-on scrambling. The route traverses the flanks of Alto de Garajonay, heads for Los Roques, runs from laurisilva forest onto scrub-covered terraces and finally descends steeply to San Sebastián.

Leave **Chipude** by following the road up to the Bar La Hoya, then up a narrow, stone-paved road. Cross the main road and keep left of a bus shelter to go down a concrete track to **Apartadero**. Turn left at the bottom, clipping a road bend, and follow a stone-paved path up to a house. Go down a narrow road and turn left up another road. Walk down to the main road and turn left to the Bar Los Camioneros. Across the road, a stony path drops into a valley, passing prickly pears and palms, rising back to the road. Turn left, then right to climb a stone-paved road through **Pavón**. A stone-paved path runs further uphill; turn right to the last house and consider climbing La Fortaleza.

The GR 131.1 passes a sign for the Monumento Natural La Fortaleza. Walk up a steep slope dotted with cistus, and crude rock-steps lead into a tight gully. There are plenty of holds for hands and feet, but ensure all moves can be reversed. At the top swing right along a ridge and cross a slight gap, reaching on the stony plateau of **La Fortaleza**. Cistus and asphodels abound and a trig point stands at 1232m (4042ft). ▸

The ascent of La Fortaleza is an optional scramble calling for a sure foot and agility

Enjoy splendid views from the summit.

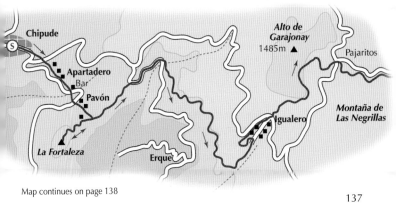

Map continues on page 138

Return to the little house above **Pavón** to follow the GR 131 up a path that is boulder-paved in places, flanked by cistus and tagasaste. When a road is reached, turn right down to a tight bend, and left as signposted for Igualero. A boulder-paved path climbs past bushy scrub, reaching pines higher up, where it becomes easier. Cross a streambed and climb further as the path gets rockier. A junction is reached where the GR 132.1 heads right (see Walk 25) and the GR 131 keeps left. Climb past terraces to a road at **Igualero**.

Turn right, then left up another road to reach the Mirador de Igualero and an ermita. Head for the main road at a bend, but turn right to follow a narrow path parallel. Reach the main road at a junction, bus shelter and map-board. Keep well left of the bus shelter to spot a sign for Alto de Garajonay. Climb past pines and laurisilva. Turn right along a track, which bends left and winds down to a road junction at **Pajaritos**.

Look for a sign for Los Roques, via Ruta 18 and GR 131, later flashed for the PR LG 15. The plain and obvious track leads to more signs, where a path on the left climbs a narrow groove on a forested slope. Log steps lead to a rocky summit. Walk down across a slight gap then up more log steps to a summit covered in cistus. The path heads down, undulating before dropping down more rugged. ◄

There is always a road to the left but it is seldom seen.

Land on a track and turn left, almost to the road, but look for a narrow, bushy path. Go up it then wind down log steps into dense forest. Climb gently to the road, walk gently up it then keep right up a heather crest, reaching the **Mirador de Tajaqué**. A stone-paved path and steps drop to the road, and the road leads to a sign for Los Roques. Use a narrow path to short-cut a road bend then walk round

Montaña de Las Negrillas

Pajaritos

Tajaqué

another bend. At a sign for Los Roques, climb a path and quickly turn left at a junction in dense forest. Visit the Mirador de Agando, or keep straight ahead down to the base of the huge **Roque de Agando**.

Cross the road and turn right to follow it, or walk beside it. When the road rises to a cutting, head left up a stone-paved path and earth steps on a slope of heather. Go through a clearing, then up and down a deeply-cut path. Reach the **Ermita de Las Nieves**, which doubles as a viewpoint, at over 1100m (3610ft).

The Roque de Agando and Benchijigua valley from a roadside mirador

Map continues on page 140

:ita

Los Roques

Roque de Agando

Ermita de Las Nieves

Degollada de Peraza

Tagamiche

Bar

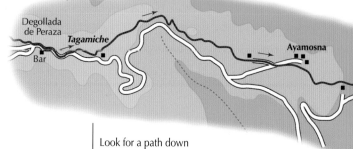

Look for a path down to its access road then walk down the road. Fork left along a track later, though a bushy and open area, past a house and a mast. Keep straight ahead and gently downhill. The track becomes a boulder-paved path down a slope of tagasaste, cistus, heather, aloes and palms, with rock-steps dropping to the main road. Turn left past a junction at **Degollada de Peraza** and pass a bus shelter and nearby bar restaurant.

The road runs through a rock cutting then a signpost points left up a concrete track. Don't climb **Tagamiche** but head right along a less obvious track. Turn left later up a broad, stone-paved track above a farm with barking dogs. Cross a boulder-paved shoulder then watch carefully to follow the path down a grassy slope. Pass a few palms and the path becomes clearer, though rugged and boulder-paved. Pass more palms and aloes on the way down to a rugged gap.

Keep right of the gap, climbing a zigzag above palms, then walk along a rocky ledge above the main road. ◄ The gradual descent is rugged underfoot, with views of the Barranco del Cabrito. Animal pens and a couple of houses are reached, so follow the access road down to a junction near **Ayamosna**.

Terraces and a couple of ruins are passed on a gradual ascent.

Just to the left of the road junction a stony track continues gently downhill. Follow it past a low cliff and it becomes very rugged further down. After a securely-fenced area, the old stone-paved path leads onwards down a crest where old terraces are covered in tabaibal. Reach a signpost beside a road and walk down the road, but use a rugged path to short-cut a bend. Follow the road past a little building, then step left onto another

140

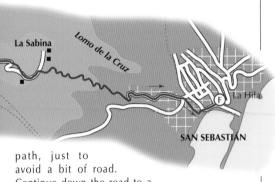

path, just to
avoid a bit of road.
Continue down the road to a
bend and keep straight ahead down a few stone steps,
following a path down to some old buildings. Turn left

*View across a rocky
gap towards Majona
on the way down from
the mountains to San
Sebastián*

141

along the road, almost to houses at **La Sabina**, over 400m (1310ft).

Turn right, as signposted, with a view of San Sebastián below while following a winding, stone-paved path down slopes of tabaibal, verode, cornical, aulaga and tamarisk. Later, wind down towards houses, turning left to reach a road at the highest house in the barranco above El Calvario. Walk down the road, Avenida de Las Galanas, to reach a new development where the road narrows. Turn left as marked, then right to continue down past a sports centre. Go down Cañada del Herrero to reach a bridge over a river near the bus station in **San Sebastián**. The GR 131 turns right to follow the river, crossing it later to pass a park, finishing on the Plaza de las Américas.

EL HIERRO

Aloes sometimes grow beside the path on the way down to
Puerto de La Estaca (Walk 45)

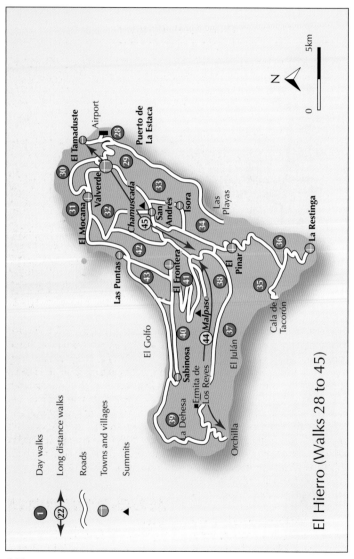

El Hierro (Walks 28 to 45)

Day walks

Long distance walks

Roads

Towns and villages

Summits

INTRODUCTION

A wonderful view of El Golfo can be enjoyed from La Peña, clouds permitting

El Hierro is the smallest and most remote of the Canary Islands, and is often overlooked. Make a visit a priority, since there is a wealth of walking opportunities. Unusually, the main settlements are located well away from the sea, with only small villages on the coast. Roads almost encircle the island and it is no longer necessary to cross the high, forested parts to link Valverde and El Frontera. Walkers can enjoy exploring traditional paths linking villages and crossing the mountains.

There are 18 days of walking on El Hierro, made up of 16 one day walks, signposted as PR (*pequeño recorrido*) routes, and a two-day walk signposted as a GR (*gran recorrido*) route, based on a traditional pilgrim trail. Very few of these routes stand in isolation, and most of them link with one, two or more adjacent routes, so there are options to alter and adapt them, and some routes feature significant variants and extensions. There are over 260km (160 miles) of walking described on El Hierro in this guidebook.

GETTING THERE

By Air

Flights from Tenerife Norte to El Hierro are operated by Binter

145

Canarias, tel. 902-391392, www.
bintercanarias.com. There are no
flights from Tenerife Sur. Buses
meet incoming flights, linking with
Valverde. Taxis are also available.

By Ferry

Two ferry companies operate between
Los Cristianos on Tenerife, and Puerto
de La Estaca on El Hierro. Lineas
Fred Olsen, tel. 902-100107, www.
fredolsen.es, is quick and expensive.
Naviera Armas, tel. 902-456500,
www.naviera-armas.com, is slower
and cheaper. Bear in mind that time-
tables are irregular and ferries do not
operate every day. Ferries are met
by buses that climb high inland to
Valverde. Taxis are also available.

GETTING AROUND

By Bus

Bus services on El Hierro have
improved dramatically in recent years.
A new fleet operates as Transportes
de Viajeros de El Hierro, shortened to
TransHierro, tel. 922-551175. There
is no website and information on the
internet is unreliable. Obtain an up-to-
date timetable for the whole island as
soon as possible, from bus stations or
tourist information offices. Flat fares for
single journeys are paid on boarding
the bus. Buses are referred to as 'guaguas', although bus stops, or *paradas*,
may be marked as 'bus'. Every village
has a bus service, operating either from
Valverde or El Frontera.

By Taxi

Taxis may be required to access walks
at the western end of El Hierro, where
there are no buses. Taxi ranks are
located at Valverde, tel. 922-551175,
and El Frontera, tel. 922-559129.
Fares are fixed by the municipalities
and can be inspected on demand,
though negotiation might be possible.

Planning your Transport

To make the most of walking opportunities, and limit long and awkward
travelling, it is best to choose a base
with good bus connections.

Linear routes described in this
book always start at the 'awkward'
end, usually high in the mountains, to
which you would need to take a taxi,
and finish where you can catch a bus.
The introduction to each walk has a
note about the availability of public
transport. If no bus is mentioned serving the start or finish, then the use of a
taxi or car will be required.

The route maps in this guide are all
at 1:200,000 scale with north to the top.

ACCOMMODATION

Accommodation is available around
El Hierro, and it is best to obtain an
up-to-date list from a tourist information office if walking from place to
place. At the top end of the scale is
the Parador at Las Playas, but there
are other hotels around the island,
as well as simple pensións and self-
catering apartments, with prices
to suit all pockets. Valverde and El

Frontera make splendid bases, not only because of the immediate variety of walks, but also because they have good bus services.

FOOD AND DRINK

El Hierro is virtually self-sufficient in terms of fruit, vegetables and fish. The island has its own 'Terencio' supermarket chain. While some restaurants are cosmopolitan, others offer good local fare. Specialities include goat cheese, which is white, smoked or cured. Wrinkly potatoes (*papas arrugadas*) cooked in salt are surprisingly refreshing in hot weather, served with hot mojo roja sauce and gentler mojo verde. The most popular fish dishes are based on vieja. If any dishes such as soups or stews need thickening, reach for the roasted flour *gofio*, which can also serve as a breakfast cereal. Local honey is branded El Tomillar, and a sweet snack called a *quesadilla* is delicious. Local wines are available, carrying the Frontera label. Never pass an opportunity to indulge in local fare!

TOURIST INFORMATION OFFICES

Valverde, tel. 922-550302
El Frontera, tel. 922-555999
La Restinga, tel. 922-557114

The Ecomuseo de Guinea is an interesting site at the foot of steep cliffs (Walk 43)

WALK 28
Valverde and La Caleta

Distance	9km (5½ miles)
Start/finish	Centre of Valverde
Total Ascent/Descent	590m (1935ft)
Time	4hrs
Terrain	Steep and stony paths on scrubby slopes.
Refreshment	Plenty of choice in Valverde. Bar at La Caleta.
Transport	Buses link Valverde with La Caleta and Puerto de La Estaca.

Two steep and rugged paths link Valverde with the coast at La Caleta. The descent follows the Camino de La Caleta, while the ascent links with the Camino Ancho, the 'broad way' that was once the main mule track between Valverde and Puerto de La Estaca.

Route uses PR EH 5.2, PR EH 5.1 and GR 131.

Start in the centre of Valverde, around 550m (1805ft), and walk down to the church. Turn left in front of it, down Calle Doctor Gost, past the Hotel Boomerang, reaching a road junction and map-board. Turn right down a steep road for La Caleta then turn right again to reach a road-end. Yellow/white markers reveal a cobbled path winding down past terraces and prickly pears. Follow an ash track

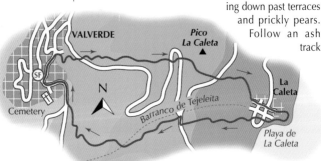

The church in the centre of Valverde, where several walking routes start and finish

past a cave and keep right along an old road to reach the main road.

Turn right down the road and left at a big cypress tree, to walk down another ash track. Turn left down an ash path that steepens on a bushy slope. Cross a road serving a water treatment works and keep straight downhill. The path levels out, descending gently beside a metal pipe and a drystone wall. The pipe turns sharp left, but keep straight ahead, rising gently. Step over another pipe and keep straight ahead, following a rough, cobbled path downhill, later fringed with aloes as it winds down to a road bend.

Cross the road and head slightly left to pick up a stretch of old road. Turn right down a cobbled path and cross the road again. A track leads quickly to gates on **Pico La Caleta**. Keep right to follow a path parallel to the track then drop steeply on bare rock. The path is cobbled later, fringed with tabaibal, with La Caleta in view. A soft ash path leads down to a road near a quarry, where coloured layers of volcanic ash can be seen.

Cross the road and walk down a winding, cobbled path, becoming a groove as it drops past tabaibal and prickly pears. A road is reached, leading straight down through **La Caleta**. Although a signpost points right along

The path climbing from La Caleta to Valverde is sometimes fringed with aloes

a road, keep straight ahead past a bar, Sabor Venezolano, and turn right at the bottom. Follow a promenade path above cliffs or go down steps to use a rugged path closer to the sea. Walk towards small swimming pools at **Playa de La Caleta**.

Climb steps from the last pool to reach a road and map-board. Climb straight up a rugged path marked for Valverde. When a road is reached, turn left along it, then right beside yellow houses, the last in La Caleta. Climb straight up a rugged path, but watch for a right turn onto an easier path, stony but not too steep, climbing beside **Barranco deTejeleita**. It is flanked by low stone walls as it passes small fields. When a road is reached, turn right to approach a junction, but turn left before it. A path climbs alongside a building and continues straight up beside a barranco, flanked by drystone walls.

A junction is reached where the PR EH 5 meets the GR 131. It is possible to turn left and follow the GR 131 to Puerto de La Estaca, ▶ but to return to Valverde, turn right. The path is broad and worn down to bare rock in many places – this is the Camino Ancho, literally the 'broad way', once the main mule track between the port and Valverde.

See Walk 45.

While climbing uphill, note the buildings across the barranco, which is a goat farm. Looking up to the skyline, a large building marks the position of Valverde, which is otherwise unseen. Avoid turnings marked 'private', and be sure to turn left at a path junction that is not too clear on the ground. Prickly pears are abundant, along with aloes and calcosas. The walled path gradually swings right, then turns left and right as it climbs, reaching a road. Turn right to follow roads into the centre of **Valverde**.

WALK 29
Valverde and Puerto de la Estaca

Distance	10km (6 miles)
Start/Finish	Centre of Valverde
Total Ascent/Descent	620m (2035ft)
Time	5hrs
Terrain	Steep and stony paths on scrubby slopes, with one descent being very steep and rocky.
Refreshment	Plenty of choice in Valverde. Bar at Puerto de La Estaca.
Transport	Buses link Valverde and Puerto de La Estaca.

Old paths and tracks link Valverde with Puerto de La Estaca. This route explores some of them, first heading downhill across the Barranco de Tiñor, then dropping very steeply to the coast. The climb from the port to Valverde links with the broad Camino Ancho,

Route uses PR EH 5, PR EH 4 and GR 131.

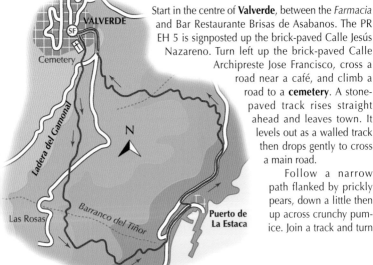

Start in the centre of **Valverde**, between the *Farmacia* and Bar Restaurante Brisas de Asabanos. The PR EH 5 is signposted up the brick-paved Calle Jesús Nazareno. Turn left up the brick-paved Calle Archipreste Jose Francisco, cross a road near a café, and climb a road to a **cemetery**. A stone-paved track rises straight ahead and leaves town. It levels out as a walled track then drops gently to cross a main road.

Follow a narrow path flanked by prickly pears, down a little then up across crunchy pumice. Join a track and turn

left to follow it, reaching a dip and a small building. Turn left down a stone-paved path flanked by water pipes, across the slopes of Ladera del Gamonal. The scrub is very mixed, with prickly pears, aloes, calcosas, tabaibal, verode and one big cypress tree.

A solitary cypress tree on the way down from Valverde to the Barranco de Tiñor

The path runs down past cultivated plots, while a few houses are seen in a valley, served by a road. The path crosses the road and follows a terrace, passing above a little *caseta* surrounded by luxuriant scrub. Cross the rocky bed of a barranco and note a peak high above. Follow the path, climbing a little, then head down to a little gate, turning right to climb again. Head down into the **Barranco de Tiñor** and turn right to walk up the rocky bed a little.

Exit left to continue up the path, passing plenty of scrub and a couple of pines. A steep and winding path levels out before heading gently down to a junction. A signpost indicates the PR EH 4, heading right up to Tiñor and left down to Puerto de La Estaca. The descent is easy at first, but steep and rugged later. The port comes into view at the same time as cardón is noticed growing on the slopes, then the path winds steeply and ruggedly further down.

153

A gentle black ash path runs down beside a wall. There is a slight climb then a red pumice path runs downhill. Pass two pylons then take care on a very steep and rocky slope. Squeeze between two houses at the foot of the slope and go down steps to a roundabout. Walk straight along a road into **Puerto de La Estaca**, where a bar is available.

Face the houses stacked against a rocky slope to find a map-board and signpost for Valverde. The stone-paved Calle García Escamez climbs between houses and the marked route swings right and left up log steps and an ash path. Pass a house and barking dogs, taking an access road up to the main road. Turn right up the bendy road, enjoying bird's-eye views of the port.

Watch for a signpost on the left for Valverde. The path makes pronounced loops as it climbs, flanked by walls and aloes as it runs at a gentler gradient to a junction with the broad Camino Ancho. Turn left to follow this uphill, and note the buildings across the barranco, which is a goat farm. Looking up to the skyline, a large building marks the position of Valverde, which is otherwise unseen. Avoid turnings marked 'private', and be sure to turn left at a path junction that is not too clear on the ground. Prickly pears are abundant, along with aloes and calcosas. The walled path gradually swings right, then turns left and right as it climbs, reaching a road. Turn right to follow roads into the centre of **Valverde**.

Looking down to Puerto de La Estaca, couched at the foot of rugged cliffs

WALK 30
Valverde, Echedo and El Mocanal

Distance	9.5km (6 miles)
Start	Centre of Valverde
Finish	El Mocanal
Total Ascent	370m (1215ft)
Total Descent	420m (1380ft)
Time	4hrs
Terrain	Steep ash slopes give way to gentle roads, tracks and paths.
Refreshment	Plenty of choice in Valverde. Bar at Echedo. Bars at El Mocanal.
Transport	Buses link Valverde with Echedo and El Mocanal.

This walk leaves Valverde and drops through vineyards on slopes of volcanic ash. After enjoying a bird's-eye view of Tamaduste the route roughly contours to Echedo, passing plenty more vineyards. There are options to extend the walk, or finish at El Mocanal.

Start in the centre of **Valverde**, around 550m (1805ft), and walk down to the church. Turn left in front of it, down Calle Doctor Gost, past the Hotel Boomerang, reaching a road junction and map-board. Walk straight ahead and continue along the level Calle la Carrera to reach a main road. Cross over and follow a narrow, brick-paved road. Turn right, then quickly left, down a road alongside a large building.

Walk off the end of the road, down a stony groove, then down log steps on a slope of black ash, passing aloes and calcosas bushes. Walk down a steep road overlooking a slope of vines. When this swings right, continue straight down a broad track on black ash, with tabaibal on either side. Reach a path junction, at 210m

Route includes GR 131, PR EH 6.2, PR EH 6.1 and PR EH 6.

155

The GR 131 heads right for El Tamaduste, while the PR EH 6.2 turns left for Echedo.

(690ft) on **Lomo de Candia**. ◄ Turn left for Echedo along a path flanked by low stone walls and calcosas. When the walls run out, crunch up a slope of black ash dotted with bushes, where the path is marked by stones bearing yellow/white flashes. Approach the red ash slopes of **La Cancela**, but swing left as marked to continue up the black ash slope. At a higher path junction, turn right to start climbing across the red ash slope.

The path levels out on a very steep slope, around 350m (1150ft), above the striking Roque Colorado. Black pumice litters the slopes of red ash, while house leeks brighten bare

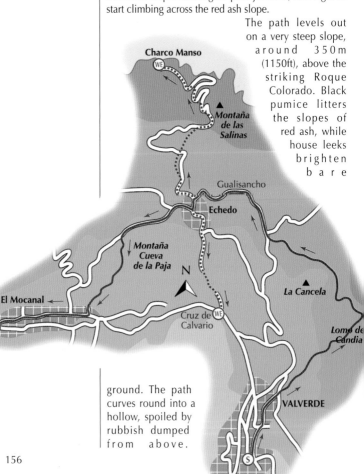

ground. The path curves round into a hollow, spoiled by rubbish dumped from above.

Beyond the hollow, a lava flow is covered in hoary lichens, ferns and house leeks, all watered by damp mists.

Another crunchy ash path meanders across terraces of vines, some of them protected by old car tyres. Cross two access tracks and keep straight ahead as marked, noting an increasing number of *casetas*. A road junction is reached on Calle Amacas. Follow the meandering road straight ahead, avoiding other roads and tracks up or down. A couple of houses sport fine cactus gardens at **Gualisancho**. A road junction is reached around 380m (1245ft) in the village of **Echedo**. ▸

See later for extension to Charco Manso and also ascent to Cruz de Calvario.

Turn left to pass a bar restaurant and walk up the road to a junction and a map-board. Turn right to follow the road signposted for El Mocanal, called Calle Simón,

The splendid old church in the village of El Mocanal sits on a new plaza

until a left turn is flashed yellow/white up a narrow road. Pass a house called La Sanjora, where there is a wine press. Follow the road and later turn left up a dirt road signposted for El Mocanal.

Do not follow the dirt road all the way to a house, but walk straight along and up a delightful winding path. This is often stone-paved, or gritty, or crosses bare rock on the slopes of **Montaña Cueva de la Paja**. Pass lots of tiny fields surrounded by drystone walls bristling with lichens. The path meanders and undulates, while other paths are marked 'X', meaning they are not to be used. A road is reached, Calle El Rincón, at some houses. Turn left uphill then turn right down another road, Calle San Pedro, gently down and up through **El Mocanal**, passing old houses and eventually reaching the main road. Hotel Villa El Mocanal, a couple of shops, bars and buses.

Extension to Charco Manso

A steep and rugged extension leads down from Echedo to the sea at Charco Manso

The PR EH 6.1 drops from Echedo to the rugged coast at Charco Manso. Bear in mind that steps have to be retraced afterwards. The distance there and back is 6km (3¾ miles), with 380m (1245ft) of descent and re-ascent.

Leave **Echedo** by road down a slope of vines and figs, continuing past old terraces covered in calcosas. Pass a small building and watch for a left turn flashed yellow/white, just before a small quarry. A worn path runs parallel to the road, downhill and well to the right of a red house. Follow a track away from the house, cross the road, and follow a path across a slope of pumice. Wind steeply down an ash slopes dotted with calcosas and tabaibal.

When the road is reached, follow it downhill, left of **Montaña de las Salinas**. Watch for a path down to the left, short-cutting the bendy road. Only one bit of road needs to be walked, then another path drops down to the left, overlooking a few *casetas*. The road is reached again at a map-board, where a left turn leads to **Charco Manso**. The low cliff coast is battered by waves, which keep clifftop pools supplied with water. ▸

By walking round the far side of a cove, a rock arch can be seen.

Ascent to Cruz de Calvario

A simple ascent of 200m (655ft) over 2km (1¼ miles) leads from Echedo to the main road at Cruz de Calvario.

Leave **Echedo** by walking straight up the road for Cruz de Calvario. Pass a bus shelter on Calle Los Valles, where there are vines on both sides of the road, and climb to the end of the tarmac at a house with a wine press. Climb a rough, stone-paved track flanked by walls and terraces of vines. The paving gives way to an ash path at Finca La Oliva, and this later joins a tarmac road. Climb steeply and pass cuttings through crumbling volcanic ash and pumice. Reach the main road at **Cruz de Calvario**. A signpost points left and right for the PR EH 6, or Camino del Norte. ▸

See Walk 31.

WALK 31
Valverde to La Peña

Distance	10km (6 miles)
Start	Centre of Valverde
Finish	Mirador de La Peña
Total Ascent	270m (885ft)
Total Descent	200m (655ft)
Time	3hrs
Terrain	Mostly easy roads, with some tracks and paths, only rarely steep.
Refreshment	Plenty of choice in Valverde. Bars at El Mocanal, Guarazoca and La Peña.
Transport	Buses link the villages with Valverde and El Frontera.

The northern part of El Hierro features a line of little villages, connected to each other and to Valverde by an old road, long since superseded by a main road. The Camino del Norte is mostly buried beneath the new road, but stretches of the old road survive.

Route uses the PR EH 6.

Follow the Calle de la Constitución through **Valverde**. This is signposted and flashed yellow/white for the PR EH 6, or Camino del Norte. Pass the post office (*Correos*) and turn left up a road for El Mocanal and La Peña. Pass the Hospital and Ermita de San Lázaro on the way out of town. Continue along the main road, on the left-hand side as marked, until approaching a bend at **Cruz de Calvario**. Switch to the right-hand side of the road to see an old wooden cross. ◄

For the link with Echido see Walk 30.

160

Follow the main road onwards, on the right-hand side, passing a couple of lay-bys and a house. Turn right as marked along a track, dropping down to a quieter road. This is the original Camino del Norte, recently resurfaced. Cross a gentle dip and rise to a small *ermita* beside **Montaña Tenesedra**. Walk down to a road junction and keep straight ahead down Calle San Pedro.

The road runs gently down and up through **El Mocanal**, passing old houses and eventually reaching the main road. Hotel Villa El Mocanal, shops, bars and buses. Walk straight ahead by road to reach the church of San Pedro and its plaza. Climb steps to leave the church, crossing a road to follow a narrow road uphill, signposted for the Camino del Norte. Climb steeply past houses with interesting gardens, avoiding turnings marked 'X', reaching the end of the tarmac at a house called **La Era**.

Follow a level track flanked by drystone walls, grassy and easy, running parallel to the main road, but well above it. Some parts are stone-paved or rocky, passing old terraces and *casetas*, some roofed and some in ruins. Join and follow a wider vehicle track above a cemetery and walk straight ahead as marked. The track rises and falls gently, then a steep concrete ramp leads

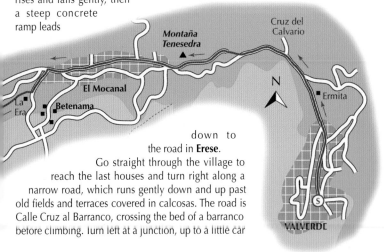

down to the road in **Erese**. Go straight through the village to reach the last houses and turn right along a narrow road, which runs gently down and up past old fields and terraces covered in calcosas. The road is Calle Cruz al Barranco, crossing the bed of a barranco before climbing. Turn left at a junction, up to a little car

A dragon tree can be seen in a garden, just off-route at Guarazoca

park, then down the road. Turn left again steeply uphill, but not up Calle la Asomada. Instead, turn right at the little Plazuela de Guarazoca.

Walk down a concrete track and continue onto a narrow tarmac road. Follow this uphill and keep left, climbing very steeply as the road gives way to a steep and rocky path. Keep climbing and keep right at junctions to reach the main road just outside **Guarazoca**. Shop, bar and buses.

There are two ways to bring this walk to a close. The quickest and easiest is to turn right and follow the road to La Peña. The other way takes a little longer, but is worth the effort. Cross the road and follow a short concrete track. Turn right along a stone-paved track flanked by drystone walls. Continue up a concrete track to reach the road. Turn right down the road, then left for the Mirador de La Peña.

Mirador de La Peña overlooks El Golfo, where half of El Hierro fell into the sea in a single cataclysmic event. The view stretches from the islets of Roques de Salmor, past El Frontera, to the distant village of Sabinosa. Sometimes El Golfo is full of cloud, while at other times the cloud hangs over Malpaso. The cliff-edge restaurant was designed by César Manrique and opened in 1989.

WALK 32
La Peña, San Andrés and El Mocanal

Distance	5km (9½ miles)
Start	Mirador de La Peña
Finish	El Mocanal
Total Ascent	480m (1575ft)
Total Descent	600m (1970ft)
Time	5hrs
Terrain	Broad dirt roads, tracks and clear paths, sometimes rocky underfoot.
Refreshment	Restaurant at La Peña. Bars at San Andrés, El Mocanal and Pozo de Las Calcosas.
Transport	Buses serve La Peña from Valverde. Buses serve San Andrés from Valverde, El Pinar and La Restinga.

The tiny Ermita de la Peña is tucked underneath a cliff and is a fine viewpoint

Enjoy the view from Mirador de La Peña then climb through a landscape criss-crossed by drystone walls to San Andrés. The route heads for Garoé and its 'holy tree', then descends to El Mocanal. Either finish there, or follow an extension down to the cliff coast.

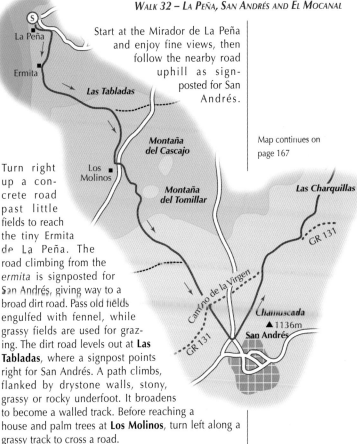

Start at the Mirador de La Peña and enjoy fine views, then follow the nearby road uphill as signposted for San Andrés.

Map continues on page 167

Turn right up a concrete road past little fields to reach the tiny Ermita de La Peña. The road climbing from the *ermita* is signposted for San Andrés, giving way to a broad dirt road. Pass old fields engulfed with fennel, while grassy fields are used for grazing. The dirt road levels out at **Las Tabladas**, where a signpost points right for San Andrés. A path climbs, flanked by drystone walls, stony, grassy or rocky underfoot. It broadens to become a walled track. Before reaching a house and palm trees at **Los Molinos**, turn left along a grassy track to cross a road.

Go straight along another track and cross a rocky streambed. Turn right to walk gently uphill beside it, then left along another walled, grassy track, winding uphill between fields. Thyme flanks the track then it passes a plantation of tagasaste. Join and follow a broad and gentle track onwards, which leads to a broad dirt road. Follow this straight ahead, crossing the **Camino de la Virgen**. ▶

See Walk 45.

The dirt road passes pines and apples, reaching a road on the outskirts of **San Andrés**. Either turn left along

A red-earth track alternates with a tarmac road, leading to the 'Árbol Garoé'

the road to continue with this walk, or head straight past the church and a map-board to reach the centre of the village, around 1050m (3445ft). Shop, bars and buses.

The continuation is signposted as the PR EH 7 to El Garoé and El Mocanal. Follow the road away from San Andrés and turn right along a dirt road for 'Árbol Garoé', between pines and eucalyptus, crossing rocky ground at the foot of **Chamuscada**. Pines flank the dirt road, with tagasaste beyond. Join another track, part of the GR 131, and follow it onwards through pine forest, entering the Paisaje Protegido Ventejís.

Low, rounded hills are volcanic ash cones. Large areas are used for grazing, but there are also remnants of laurisilva.

◄ When a junction is reached, turn left up a steep road for 'Árbol Garoé', which becomes a dirt road, passing a sign at **Las Charquillas**, over 1100m (3610ft). The dirt road runs past patchy laurisilva then a steep road drops to a reception centre for **Árbol Garoé**.

The **'holy tree'** at Garoé was revered by the Bimbaches of El Hierro. It was a mighty tree that once towered above extensive forest, sieving mist and dripping water onto the ground. Channels and cisterns were cut to catch and store the water. The tree fell during a hurricane in 1610, and its replacement will take centuries to mature.

Walk down a concrete ramp and follow a clear, red-earth track winding down beside a valley full of laurisilva and aloes. The track passes eroded areas and becomes steeper, covered in loose pumice, but a firmer track is joined, featuring parallel strips of concrete. Follow it down to a junction and keep straight ahead, then follow a track running left of a gate.

An easy stretch flanked by fennel is followed by another steep slope covered in pumice and ash. A rugged stone-paved path threads its way between old fields of fennel. When a road is reached, turn left and almost immediately right, to walk down a rugged path on a slope of prickly pears. Another road is reached at **Betenama**; follow it steeply downhill to reach the main road through **El Mocanal**. Hotel Villa El Mocanal, shops, bars and buses.

Extension to Pozo de Las Calcosas

This spur runs to the cliff coast at Pozo de las Calcosas. The distance there-and-back is 12km (7½ miles), with 500m (1640ft) of descent and re-ascent.

Leave the Supermercado Marielly in **El Mocanal**, cross the road and walk down to Calle San Pedro. Turn right, then left for Calle Los Almendreros, signposted for Pozo de Las Calcosas. The road gives way to a rough-paved path flanked by walls. Drop downhill, sometimes on bare rock, other times stony underfoot, while slopes alongside feature citrus, then almonds, prickly pears and calcosas. Wind downhill past ruined casetas near an old pylon.

Note the abundance of aloes, tabaibal and verode on the slope.

Cross a road and continue straight down a path. Pass a house where there is rampant vegetation. ◀ Continue downhill in a broad loop and reach a road, Camino de Tancajote. Walk straight down past a pizzería and bars, to reach an *ermita* and a *mirador* at the road-end. Look down on a huddle of thatched huts. Go down a winding, stone-paved path, Camino de las Calcosas, and pick a way between the huts at **Pozo de Las Calcosas** to reach rock pools and a bathing pool. Steps have to be retraced all the way uphill afterwards.

A lengthy extension runs from El Mocanal to the sea at Pozo de Las Calcosas

WALK 33

Puerto de la Estaca, La Cuesta and Tiñor

Distance	14km (8¾ miles)
Start/Finish	Puerto de La Estaca
Total Ascent/Descent	1000m (3280ft)
Time	5hrs
Terrain	Road-walking at the top and bottom, with tracks and paths on the ascent and descent, sometimes steep and rugged.
Refreshment	Bars at Puerto de La Estaca and Timijiraque.

Steep, rugged, scrub-covered slopes rise above the coast road linking Puerto de la Estaca and Timijiraque. A path climbs to La Cuesta, and another path leads towards Tiñor, while a final path allows a steep and rugged descent to return to the port.

Leave **Puerto de La Estaca** to pass a roundabout and follow the coast road for Timijiraque. Pass a **power station** and later reach a tunnel. Keep left to follow the old coast road and beware of rock-falls. At the other end of the tunnel a sculpture bears the words '*Te esperaré siempre...*' ('I'll wait for you forever...') A promenade path runs round a small ash beach, and the road leads onwards into **Timijiraque**. Bars and buses.

Route uses PR EH 4 and PR EH 5.

A signpost beside a map-board indicates the PR EH 4 for La Cuesta, where a concrete road leaves the main road and enters the Paisaje Protegido Timijiraque. Climb to a house and continue up a track flanked by walls and incienso, with cardón at a higher level. Pass a concrete water store where a stony path flanked by walls climbs past old fields and terraces. The path zigzags uphill where the scrub includes verode, tabaibal and cornical.

Cross a road and continue up the stony path. Pass bushy tabaibal and later cross a dirt road. Keep climbing as the path broadens, crossing the road again. Further uphill, cistus grows among the scrub and there is a solitary juniper. Climb beside a rugged lava flow, with the striking peaks of **Montaña de la Fortaleza** to the left. Climb a vague path and follow it onto the surface of the lava flow, watching for yellow/white flashes and little cairns.

Climb to cross the road again, then the path is clearer as it crosses the road soon after. On the next ascent the path is less clear on bare rock, levelling out parallel to the road, where dense scrub includes prickly pears.

The route runs up Calle Jineque to leave the tiny settlement of La Cuesta

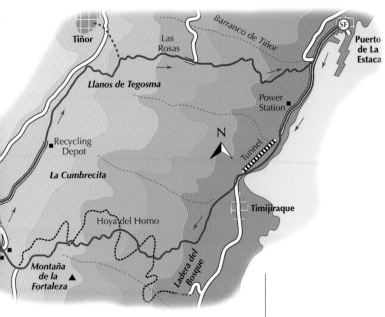

Reach a dry streambed above a rocky gorge and turn right to walk up the bed, exiting left along a walled path. Zigzag up past tagasaste, crossing the road again. The walled path climbs, zigzagging with a stone-paved or rocky surface, to reach houses. Turn left up the concrete Calle La Esperilla to reach a crossroads at **La Cuesta**.

Walk through the crossroads and go up Calle Jineque, signposted for San Andrés. Just after the first house a sign-post points straight ahead for Puerto de la Estaca and the route soon re-joins the main road. Turn left, then right by road, passing prickly pears and tagasaste. Keep right at a junction to pass a water treatment plant. Later, there are unsightly waste recycling compounds. Turn left down a road to pass a graveyard for old cars, and left down a track to reach a big building.

Turn left along an undulating walled path, where cultivated trees have gone rampant. Walk along a rea-sonably easy track and later turn right to drop steeply down another walled path. Tree scrub gives way to fennel and other scrub, where sheep and goats graze. The path becomes rugged and swings left to pass above two cypress trees that look like one large tree.

Turn right downhill, then left to reach a signpost at a junction. Turning left offers an opportunity to climb to the village of **Tiñor**, but the route turns right downhill as signposted for Puerto de la Estaca. The narrow, walled path passes prickly pears and tabaibal. Follow it and avoid all paths marked 'X'. Reach a shady cypress tree with bathtubs beside it, then walk down a narrow road until it bends sharply left. ◄

The road runs to Valverde.

Walk down a grassy, walled path to a junction where the PR EH 4 links with the PR EH 5. Keep right and the descent is easy at first, but steep and rugged later. The port comes into view at the same time as cardón is noticed growing on the slopes; the path then winds steeply and ruggedly further down.

A gentle black ash path runs down beside a wall. There is a slight climb then a red pumice path runs downhill. Pass two pylons then take care on a very steep and rocky slope. Squeeze between two houses at the foot of the slope and go down steps to a roundabout. Walk straight along a road into **Puerto de La Estaca**, where a bar is available.

The PR EH 4 intersects with the PR EH 5 near the Barranco de Tiñor

WALK 34

Mirador de Isora and Las Playas

Distance	15km (9½ miles)
Start/Finish	Mirador de Isora
Total Ascent/Descent	1150m (3775ft)
Time	6hrs 30min
Terrain	Steep and rugged paths need great care on the descent and ascent. Easy roads and tracks at the bottom and top.
Refreshment	Bars off-route at Isora, Las Playas and Las Casas.
Transport	Buses serve Mirador de Isora and Las Playas from Valverde. Buses also serve Las Casas from Valverde, San Andrés and La Restinga.
Note	Some parts are unsuitable for vertigo sufferers.

People visit the Mirador de Isora and the Mirador de Las Playas, enjoying splendid views over cliffs protected as the Monumento Natural Las Playas. There are steep, winding paths running down and up the cliffs for anyone with a good head for heights.

Start at the **Mirador de Isora**, and go down stone steps onto stone-paved platforms to look down precipitous slopes to the sea over 830m (2725ft) below. Climb back up the steps and turn left as marked by yellow/white flashes, entering the Monumento Natural Las Playas.

The path is flanked by stone walls, crossing a slight dip before starting its long descent. ▶ Take the descent slowly and steadily. A big lump of rock is passed at **Lomo Justa**. Wind downhill and go through a gateway. Vista El Pozo offers a sudden precipitous view to the shore. Another feature is Cueva Los Ajos, a large cave on the descent. A rocky outcrop is passed at **La Charca**, then the path drops into a rocky barranco.

Route uses PR EH 3.

The steep slope looks like a botanical garden with trees and flowery scrub.

A view across a rocky gap half-way down the rugged path to Las Playas

Watch carefully for markers and climb across chunky scree to a gap above the barranco. Climb a little higher then follow the path down a scrubby slope. Leave the Monumento Natural Las Playas to reach a signpost on a narrow road and turn left downhill. The road offers an easy descent; yellow/white markers indicate a streambed to the left, but this is awkward. Either way, reach the coast road at **Las Playas**. Turn left if a bar is required, otherwise turn right to reach the luxury **Parador** hotel.

Pass the hotel and a few houses, marvelling at cactus gardens. Look uphill to spot masses of cardón, appropriately growing at **Los Cardónes**. Follow the road uphill almost to the last house. Go through a gate and re-enter the Monumento Natural Las Playas. ◄ Masses of plants grow on old terraces, changing as progress is made uphill. Cardón gives way to juniper bushes after the first pylon.

Electricity pylons march up a very steep and scrubby slope.

The path wriggles up a steep, rocky, scrubby ridge, with cistus common as the path comes level with the second pylon, where there are also a few pines. The path has been hammered from rock as it climbs past the third pylon. Notice a rock arch beside the path below the fourth

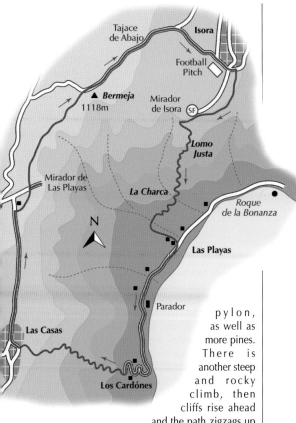

pylon, as well as more pines. There is another steep and rocky climb, then cliffs rise ahead and the path zigzags up to the right. Cistus becomes bushier among the pines, while the path follows a fence as it runs level with the fifth pylon.

Go through a gate to climb past pines and the path levels out near the sixth pylon. There is a gentle ascent past old terraces. Walk up a dry streambed, but watch for a path marked off to the left, which leads to a road and houses at **Las Casas**. Turn right up Calle El Leon to reach a crossroads. Bar and buses on a nearby main road. Turn

175

After an easy road walk at Las Playas, the route climbs back up the cliffs

right as signposted for Isora, walking up Calle La Pasada, until a slight dip in the road crosses a streambed. Turn left up a walled, grassy, cobbled track. This soon re-joins the road, but is a fine bit of old highway. Follow the road up past almonds and figs, to more pines.

Before reaching a farm, turn right at a big eucalyptus, then left up a path beside fenced fruit and vegetables. Walk along a path among pines to reach a road. Turn right to **Mirador de Las Playas** for a fine view over the cliffs. To continue the walk, however, cross the road as signposted. A grassy track leads onwards, rocky in places, passing pines and heather trees. Later, it passes tagasaste and crosses a couple of streambeds. Join and follow a track clinging to the cliff edge, then join a road and follow it up to a junction. Turn right to pass a hump of quarried red ash at **Bermeja**, whose 1118m (3668ft) summit is easily gained.

Walk down the road past dense tagasaste, passing little farms around **Tajace de Abajo**. Turn right down a road leading to a staggered crossroads beside a **football pitch**. ◄ Go through the crossroads and down Calle

Turning left leads to Isora and a bar.

Los Valles. Turn right at the bottom to follow a walled, grassy track past old fields grown rampant with bushes. The path runs parallel to a road and both lead to the **Mirador de Isora**.

Paths run up and down the cliffs above Las Playas on El Hierro

177

WALK 35

El Pinar to Cala de Tacorón

Distance	8km (5 miles)
Start	Taibique, El Pinar
Finish	Cala de Tacorón
Total	Ascent 50m (165ft)
Total	Descent 900m (2950ft)
Time	3hrs
Terrain	Mostly down good tracks and paths, occasionally steep and rugged.
Refreshment	Bars at El Pinar. Café at Cala de Tacorón.
Transport	Buses serve El Pinar from Valverde, San Andrés and La Restinga.

This fine walk runs mostly downhill from El Pinar, through rugged volcanic landscapes, to the coast at Cala de Tacorón. Bear in mind that there are no buses at the finish, and if a lift cannot be arranged then it is necessary to walk to the nearest bus route. It may be possible, by prior arrangement, to get a taxi back from Cala de Tacorón.

Route uses PR EH 1.1.

Hotel El Pinar, shops, bars, post office, banks with ATMs, buses. Start on the little plaza at **Taibique** in El Pinar and, if there is time, visit the Centro de Interpretación Parque Rural Cabecera Sur to discover more about the surrounding countryside. A map-board and a signpost indicate the PR EH 1.1, or Camino de Tacorón. Follow a road past the post office (*Correos*), up and downhill, leaving the village along a dirt road. Turn left at a junction down a walled path signposted for Tacorón. The slopes support all kinds of fruit and nuts. Walk down to the main road and follow it gently downhill, turning right along a road signposted for **Las Lapas**.

F
Cala
Taco.

Baked clay where seasonal flooding occurs near the rugged volcanic cone of Roque Grande

After only a short way, turn left down a track to a lower road. Turn right, gently down into a dip to pass lots of vines then climb a short way up the road. Turn left along a walled track, passing a couple of ash cones at **Tembargena**, dropping through vineyards dotted with figs. The track becomes more rugged as it descends through fields colonised by calcosas, verode and tabaibal.

Land on a broad dirt road and turn right gently downhill. Pass a goat farm and a quarry. Watch for a left turn down a steep and loose ash track on a scrubby slope, becoming firm and gentle later. Continue down to a track at a small electricity substation and turn right. ▶ The track leaves the substation and crosses a level area which can flood after heavy rain. Reach a ramshackle **farmstead** and turn left. A walled ash track descends gently and easily down a slope of broken lava, dotted with calcosas, verode and tabaibal. It becomes stony later and passes a

Roque Grande is just off-route, a rugged volcanic cone quite unlike the gentle ash cones nearby.

179

Savage terrain around Cala de Tacorón can be explored using short paths

couple of cypress trees. The track later breaks up and becomes very rugged. When the wall on the right drifts to the right, follow it to pick up a narrow path, flashed yellow/white. This is quite easy later, threading its way through jagged lava and scrub. Descend and level out, passing figs and prickly pears to reach a gate onto a road. The crater of **El Calderetón** is just across the road.

Turn right as signposted for Tacorón. A crunchy ash path heads down to the left, clipping a road bend, then log steps lead down a steep ash slope. Follow the road down to a car park and café. The rugged **Cala de Tacorón** is a popular swimming spot, while a red track and a black path can be used to explore the coast either side, but beware of rock-falls and landslides.

Anyone unable to arrange a pick-up must retrace their steps and head for a distant road junction to catch one of the buses linking La Restinga and El Pinar. The distance is 4km (2½ miles).

WALK 36
El Pinar to La Restinga

Distance	9km (5½ miles)
Start	Taibique, El Pinar
Finish	La Restinga
Total Ascent	50m (165ft)
Total Descent	900m (2950ft)
Time	3hrs
Terrain	Mostly easy roads, tracks and paths, but some paths are rugged.
Refreshment	Bars at El Pinar and La Restinga.
Transport	Buses serve El Pinar and La Restinga from San Andrés and Valverde.

This route runs directly south from El Pinar to reach La Restinga. Cultivated slopes below the village are planted with vines, but as the walk progresses the terrain features plenty of scrub, bleak and barren lava flows and extensive slopes of volcanic ash.

Start on the little plaza at **Taibique** in El Pinar (Hotel El Pinar, shops, bars, post office, banks with ATMs, buses) and, if there is time, visit the Centro de Interpretación Parque Rural Cabecera Sur to discover more about the surrounding countryside. A map-board and a signpost indicate the PR EH 1, or Camino de la Restinga. Walk straight down a narrow road, past the Iglesia de San Antonio Abad and its little plaza. Go down to a staggered crossroads and turn right, marked 'no entry'. Follow the road straight ahead, down towards a **cemetery**.

Turn left just before the cemetery, signposted Camino de la Restinga, down a walled track past small fields at **La Rocha**. Cross the main road and short-cut a bend. Turn right along a road signposted for El Cascajo, passing

Route uses PR EH 1.

181

Looking down scrubby slopes to volcanic ash cones above La Restinga

grassy, scrubby fields. Turn left as marked down a walled track to a house at Finca Camila. Walk straight along a vehicle track, passing vines, then straight past a white house, avoiding tracks to the left and right. Walk down past one last plantation of vines, then the track drops rugged and stone-paved.

Keep straight ahead along the broadest track, becoming broad and dusty as it levels out, then drop to a vehicle track near **Montaña La Lajura**. Turn right, in effect straight ahead, from ash slopes onto blocky lava covered in bushy scrub. The track bends left and right, then leave it to follow a walled path downhill, crunching on dark pumice. Parts of the ash path are level and easy, but later it becomes narrow and rocky as it descends. There is another easy stretch before crossing the main road. Pass a Camino de la Restinga sign then cross a narrow road.

Pick up and follow a walled track with a water pipe beside it. Bushy tabaibal and lavender flank the track and conditions underfoot are rugged. An agricultural plot is reached on the slopes of **Montaña del Jable**. Walk down the access track on crunchy ash. Turn quickly right and left at a track junction and continue along the track with a water pipe beside it. Rectangular walled enclosures are arranged on the right while, on the left, slopes of black volcanic ash are dotted with aromatic incienso, tabaibal, verode and calcosas. Keep following the track and water pipe to pass beneath a pylon line.

Keep to the yellow/white flashed path on the final descent, passing a waterworks and avoiding tracks that loop and take too long to walk. Reach a road junction at the top of **La Restinga**, beside a map-board and bus shelter. Walk straight down an attractive, narrow street to reach the little harbour. Despite a long fishing history, the village is quite modern, with a fine stone promenade and a massive sea-wall. Apartments, pensión, bank with ATM, post office, shops, bars, restaurants and buses. There are several diving centres (centros de buceo) and a tourist information office, tel. 922-557114.

The harbour in the village of La Restinga on the southernmost point of El Hierro

WALK 37
Ermita de Los Reyes to El Pinar

Distance	17.5km (11 miles)
Start	Ermita de Los Reyes
Finish	Taibique, El Pinar
Total Ascent	550m (1805ft)
Total Descent	400m (1310ft)
Time	6hrs
Terrain	Mostly good tracks and paths, though some are vague and rugged. Some lengthy road-walking.
Refreshment	Bars at El Pinar.
Transport	Buses serve El Pinar from Valverde, San Andrés and La Restinga.

The Ermita de Los Reyes was dedicated in 1577 and houses a statue of the Virgin

The western end of El Hierro, La Dehesa, was used mainly by shepherds from El Pinar, who drove animals along the Camino de los Pastores, at a general altitude of 900m (2950ft). It is best to arrange a lift or taxi to Los Reyes and walk back to El Pinar.

Leave the **Ermita de Los Reyes**, walk up a road alongside, then along a dirt road to a complex junction, map-board and signposts at Piedra del Regidor. Climb straight ahead to reach a cross-track and turn right as signposted for the Camino de los Pastores. The walled track passes juniper and scrub-covered fields. Go down through a gateway into a forest, following the track to a road bend on the slopes of **Montaña Tembargena**.

Turn left up the road to reach a gate on the right. Follow a dirt road gently downhill until it swings right towards a reservoir. Watch for a path leaving the bend, flashed yellow/white, climbing easily through tabaibal. Reach a small gate in a wall and go through. Turn left to walk parallel to the wall, through tabaibal and thyme, watching for markers. Follow a track away from a gate, but not too far. Watch for a marker and walk parallel to the wall. The path becomes rugged, crossing ravines and climbing past rocky lumps, over a rocky lip into a shallow crater at **Hoya de Los Carites**. ▶

Continue up the path to a rugged track and climb between a reservoir and a water trough to reach a wall. Turn right to follow a path parallel to the wall. Uphill on the left are pines and a road while down to the right are junipers, thyme and tabaibal. Walk ahead and later drift right down a slope of loose ash, watching for markers, and pass a water trough on a scrubby ash slope.

Swing left a couple of times when markers are spotted, crossing a ravine cut into pumice. Wind across a scrubby slope, passing junipers on a stony, gritty path, except where shallow barrancos

Route uses PR EH 10.

Huge tabaibal grows here; a little lava tube can be inspected, and there is a walled-off cave.

Map continues on page 186

GR131

(S) Ermita de Los Reyes

▲ *Montaña Tembargena*

Hoya de Los Carites

El Tomillar

185

El Tomillar

Camino de Los Pastores

Las Laderas

Visitor Centre

Parque Cultural El Julán

Archaeological Zone

feature
bare rock.
More and more pines
grow and the path eventually reaches a **visitor centre**

*Watching for yellow/
white markers while
walking across scrubby
slopes to El Julán*

186

for the Parque Cultural El Julán. Walkers arriving early can join a guided tour to inspect carvings made by the Bimbaches of El Hierro. Unaccompanied visits are not allowed. ▸ Follow the access

In 1873 and 1874 two brothers discovered Los Letreros (the letters) and Los Números (the numbers) carved on lava flows far below.

Lomo Verde

N

La Asomada ■ Hut

Montaña La Empalizada

road away from the visitor centre, uphill and over a crest beside a tall wall, reaching a road junction, map-board and signpost. Turn right to follow the road across the forested slope, undulating gently. A dirt road later climbs sharp left for Mercadel and Cruz de los Reyes, but stay on the tarmac road

Map continues on page 188

An ash track between forest and fields near Montaña La Empalizada

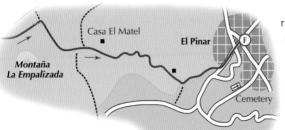

A junction is reached at **La Asomada** where a dirt road slants down to the right, for Casita El Llano, signposted for the PR EH 10. Follow it, with pines to the left and figs dotted around fields to the right. When the dirt road swings right at a concrete **hut**, keep left and follow an ash track gently uphill, crossing a gap beside **Montaña La Empalizada**. Pass a little house, where more figs are planted, and eventually reach a junction with a dirt road.

Turn right to follow the dirt road as signposted for Taibique, with walls alongside as it passes almonds, figs and prickly pears. There are tall pines, then the road runs through a vineyard. Pass the access track for **Casa El Matel**, climb past pines, then head down and up through cuttings in ash and pumice. Walk down past a house and turn left at a junction. Pass little houses and farms, and a signpost for the Camino de Tacorón (see Walk 35). Follow the road uphill and keep left at a junction, crossing a crest to walk down past the post office (*Correos*) onto a plaza in the centre of **El Pinar**.

WALK 38

El Pinar to Sabinosa

Distance	16km (10 miles)
Start	Taibique, El Pinar
Finish	Sabinosa
Total Ascent	670m (2100ft)
Total Descent	1190m (3905ft)
Time	6hrs
Terrain	Steep roads, forest tracks and mountain paths on the ascent; steep forested slopes with steep and rugged paths on the descent.
Refreshment	Bars at El Pinar. Bar at Sabinosa.
Transport	Buses serve El Pinar from Valverde, San Andrés and La Restinga. Buses serve Sabinosa from El Frontera.

This walk is based on a track that was once the only practical link between El Pinar and Sabinosa. The ascent is through pine forest, followed by a traverse across the ash slopes of Malpaso. The descent is through lush laurisilva, finishing on steep cultivated slopes.

Start on the little plaza at **Taibique** in El Pinar. Hotel El Pinar, shops, bars, post office, banks with ATMs, buses. A map-board and a signpost on the plaza indicate the PR EH 1, climbing a road beside the Bar El Mentidero to the Plaza de San Esteban. Keep right and climb further to reach a junction of five roads at **Tejina**. Left is for a *mirador* at Tanajara, while the next road runs up beside a streambed, flashed yellow/white.

Climb past fields to a road junction and walk straight up a walled track, past a notice for the Parque Rural El Frontera. Follow the track up into pine forest and keep left twice as marked, avoiding a large building. Curious columnar cairns lead to a signpost where a left turn leads

Route uses PR EH 1.

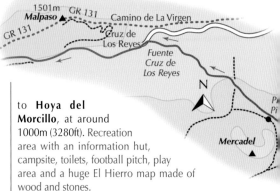

Map continues on
page 193

to **Hoya del Morcillo**, at around 1000m (3280ft). Recreation area with an information hut, campsite, toilets, football pitch, play area and a huge El Hierro map made of wood and stones.

The descent to Sabinosa runs through dense laurisilva cloud forest

Follow a fence from the map of El Hierro to a map-board at a road junction, where there is a large sign for Hoya del Morcillo. Walk straight ahead, signposted for Sabinosa, up a path and track in a sunken hollow. Turn left along a clear track, undulating but generally

climbing more than it falls. Avoid a bulldozed track to the right, keeping left to pass a sign for **Cueva El Mocán**. ▸ Keep left at a fork, following a long track with no markers. When yellow/white markers appear later, turn right and follow a stony track uphill. (If you miss it, the main track meets it later.) A junction is reached at **Pino Piloto**, a big pine tree burnt through its middle, yet still flourishing.

An interesting lava tube whose main shaft is barred by a gate.

Another tree has water taps around it. Keep right of both trees and rise gently to another junction. ▸ Walk straight uphill past more huge pines, as well as heather trees. Reach a junction at Fuentes del Julán. Turn right as signposted for Sabinosa and the track becomes steep and rutted. Watch for an ash path off to the left, leading into laurisilva. This leads into a damp forested valley full of steps and water taps at **Fuente Cruz de Los Reyes**. Climb to a junction of tarmac roads, where a signpost points straight ahead for Sabinosa.

Look around to spot some enormous multi-trunked pines.

When the tarmac ends continue along a dirt road and climb past replanted laurisilva to reach a junction. Keep straight ahead as signposted for Sabinosa, passing laurisilva and pines, as well as a concrete reservoir. Keep left at a junction, where a right turn could be used to climb **Malpaso**. ▸

Highest point on El Hierro, at 1501m (4925ft), climbed on Walk 44.

After passing the turning, take the next right turn, following a track across a bare slope of ash. Pass some

191

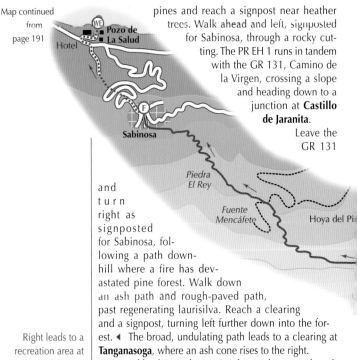

Map continued
from
page 191

pines and reach a signpost near heather trees. Walk ahead and left, signposted for Sabinosa, through a rocky cutting. The PR EH 1 runs in tandem with the GR 131, Camino de la Virgen, crossing a slope and heading down to a junction at **Castillo de Jaranita**.

Leave the GR 131 and turn right as signposted for Sabinosa, following a path downhill where a fire has devastated pine forest. Walk down an ash path and rough-paved path, past regenerating laurisilva. Reach a clearing and a signpost, turning left further down into the forest. ◄ The broad, undulating path leads to a clearing at **Tanganasoga**, where an ash cone rises to the right.

Right leads to a recreation area at Hoya del Pino.

Head back into dense pine forest, then an ash path leads down through laurisilva, followed by boulder-paved stretches and occasional clearings. Pass a notice for the Reserva Natural Integral Mencáfete and continue downhill. The path winds in dark, dense laurisilva and eventually a dirt road is reached. Turn left to reach a tarmac road, then left again up a track signposted as the Camino Sabinosa.

When another signpost is reached, climbing further uphill leads to **Fuente Mencáfete**, but steps need to be retraced. Instead, turn right for Sabinosa. The path is flanked by heather trees and tangled scrub, reaching a junction. Keep straight ahead, passing a mass of brambles, while heather trees give way to a scrubby slope dominated by calcosas. Leave the Reserva Natural Integral Mencáfete at **Piedra El Rey**.

A winding ash path becomes stony and uneven. Heather trees give way to juniper on the scrubby slope, while vines feature later. A broad ash path and winding boulder path lead onto a slope of ash, where the route leaves the Parque Rural Frontera. The path is broad and easy as it reaches houses at **Sabinosa**. Walk straight ahead along a road, then right down a tarmac road and finish in the little plaza in the village. Shop, bar and buses.

Extension to Pozo de La Salud

Leave Sabinosa along the bendy road for the coast, but watch for a path on the right across ash slopes. Cross the road three

times while descending the path, then cross a pipeline. Go straight down a steep road, which becomes gentler, to reach the main road. Turn left for the spa hotel at **Pozo de La Salud** and explore the cliff coast. The extension measures 2km (1¼ miles) with a descent of 300m (985ft).

WALK 39
La Dehesa Circuit

Distance	11km (7 miles)
Start/Finish	Ermita de Los Reyes
Total Ascent/Descent	400m (1310ft)
Time	3hrs
Terrain	Mostly along an easy dirt road and tracks, but some paths are steep and vague. The link route is steep and rugged.
Refreshment	Bar at Sabinosa on the link route.
Transport	Buses serve Sabinosa from El Frontera, on the link route.

La Dehesa is the remote western end of El Hierro, arid and unpopulated, but important for grazing livestock. Ancient, twisted, gnarled, weather-beaten junipers (*sabinas*) grow at El Sabinal. These can be reached by driving along a dirt road, but there is also a fine walk.

Route uses PR EH 9. Link route uses PR EH 9.2.

Leave the **Ermita de Los Reyes**, walk up a road alongside, then along a dirt road to a complex junction, map-board and signposts at **Piedra del Regidor**. Simply turn left to follow the dirt road for El Sabinal. The road is flanked by terraces, then pines. After passing close to a water trough it climbs gently with pines on the right and junipers on the left. After an avenue of cypress trees, the road runs gently down past open fields. Turn left at a junction as signposted for El Sabinal.

Follow the road down and sharp left, then gradually right. Cushion-like junipers are dotted around the slopes, while further downhill there are lots of old gnarled specimens. The road leads to a car park and map-boards at **El Sabinal**, where a notice explains about the junipers. ◄

A short circular walk, measuring only 4km (2½ miles), starts here.

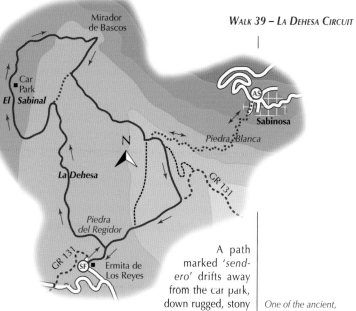

A path marked 'sendero' drifts away from the car park, down rugged, stony dusty slopes, overlooking lots of twisted junipers. A signpost confirms this as the PR EH 9. Follow the path past dense cistus, then drift uphill

One of the ancient, gnarled, twisted junipers (sabinas) at El Sabinal

195

as marked by wooden pegs. The path rises and falls, meandering across the slope, but mostly climbs. Cross a track and climb a path between a rocky rib and pine trees. Wind-blasted pines grow further uphill then there is just a rocky slope.

Turn left along a dirt road to reach the **Mirador de Bascos**, where there is a splendid bird's-eye view of Sabinosa and El Golfo. Walk back along the road, into pine forest then out into a broad clearing, to another signpost. ◄ Turn left as signposted for Sabinosa, up a stony, dusty path, passing between the forest and old fields to reach a gate and steps.

A short-cut is possible, following the road onwards, turning right at a junction to return to El Sabinal.

A steep, walled track features more steps, climbing past old fields until there is a cliff on the left. Heather trees grow along the edge and the track climbs to a junction. It is possible to turn right here and save a bit of height, but keep left and climb to a map-board to study options for a future visit. Of particular note is a path heading left for the village of Sabinosa (see below).

To finish this walk, keep right and follow the track signposted as the PR EH 9, which is partly grassy, passing bushes, scrub and old fields. The track undulates, but

An obvious walled track climbs through fields to reach a cliff edge before the descent

generally runs downhill, with junipers plentiful by the time it reaches a cross-track. Turn right to walk downhill, passing the complex junction at **Piedra del Regidor** to finish back at the **Ermita de Los Reyes**.

Link Route from Sabinosa

Walkers using buses can reach La Dehesa by climbing the steep and rugged path from Sabinosa. The distance one-way is 3km (2 miles), with an ascent of 600m (1970ft), which must be taken into account if returning.

Start on the plaza in **Sabinosa**, where a signpost indicates the Ermita de los Reyes. Walk up Calle del Moral and turn right up the steeper Camino La Dehesa, levelling out above houses. A signpost points left for the Camino de La Dehesa. Follow the winding, stone-paved path uphill, past a notice for the Parque Rural Frontera. Pass a stone seat at El Descansadero and keep winding up a slope of scrub and junipers, later passing **Piedra Blanca**.

As the path climbs, heather trees are seen and, after passing a notice for the Reserva Natural Integral Mencáfete, they dominate other scrub, before laurisilva is entered. Climb further and pass through a rocky gap. Climb less steeply, even levelling out, where the path cuts into ash and pumice. The trees thin and there are views before the path leaves the Reserva Natural Integral Mencáfete. After turning a corner the PR EH 9 is joined at a track above La Dehesa.

WALK 40

Sabinosa to El Frontera

Distance	12km (7½ miles)
Start	Sabinosa
Finish	El Frontera
Total	Ascent 200m (655ft)
Total	Descent 150m (490ft)
Time	3hrs 15 min
Terrain	A broad and easy track, except for a steep descent at the start and a steep ascent at the finish.
Refreshment	Bars at Sabinosa. Bar off-route at Los Llanillos. Bars at El Frontera.
Transport	Buses link Sabinosa, Los Llanillos and El Frontera.

The steep slopes of ash near the village of Sabinosa are wonderfully fertile, but need to be watered. A water channel (*canal*) was constructed from El Frontera to Sabinosa, but now lies in ruins. However, it is accompanied by a broad track that offers an easy walk.

Route uses PR EH 2.3.

Start on the plaza in **Sabinosa** and follow Calle de Dolores Perez Ayala, signposted as the PR EH 2.3. The road drops straight down through the village and a steep, rugged path drops down a scrubby slope, landing on a broad gravel track, Pista del Canal. Turn right to follow the track and old pipeline, crossing

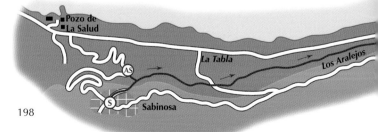

198

a steep slope covered in tabaibal, verode and calcosas, while rock-faces are studded with house leeks.

Follow the track past a pylon, where another track rises from a farm. Continue across an ash slope covered in vines and pass a water tank to reach a road. The pipeline crosses a rocky barranco on stilts, so turn right up the road, then left down a track to join it again. Cornical covers the slope, then the pipeline gives way to a concrete box channel. Keep following the track and there is an ash cone ahead, **Montaña Tamasina**, crowned with a pylon.

The track beside the canal is level and easy, despite the steepness of the slopes

Map continues on page 200

199

The track turns round a hollow used as a dump, while later a solitary juniper rises above, before a house is passed. Curve round a hollow planted with pineapples. Cross a road to find the marked route past the lowest houses in **Los Llanillos**. When a signpost is reached, the PR EH 2.2 can be followed right up into the village, or left down to Charco Azul. ◄

See extension below.

Continue along the track, crossing a road and passing a curious house. Pass a water store and later a couple of pineapple plots. Follow the track across scrubby slopes and pass the walled garden of a house, La Rayuela. ◄ Pass a house with a fine garden, cross a road and follow a level road to a junction.

Note the track leading to Miraflores Ottlik, where there is luxurious greenery.

Keep straight ahead along a road signposted for Las Lapas. Pass a large **reservoir** and go straight through a crossroads. There are more houses and more cultivated areas, but still plenty of calcosas. Cross a main road, where there is a bar and a chance to sample quesadillas at La Herreña. Keep straight ahead through a complex intersection to pick up the channel beyond, where scrub-covered slopes flank the track.

Walk 42 allows an extension to Guinea and Las Puntas.

The bendy track leads to **Las Lapas**, where there is a crossroads. ◄ Turn right up a steep road, then left up a steeper stone-paved road. Turn right up a tarmac road and climb past the little plaza at Calle La Cruz. Walk up through a crossroads and climb the steepening Calle Las Lapas. Vines grow on the slopes and the road is stone-paved up to a junction at **El Frontera**.

Of immediate interest are the Canarian wrestling arena (Campo de Lucha) and the Iglesia de Nuestra Señora De Candelaria, dating from 1615, as well as a bar and buses. If the road is followed down into town there are more facilities.

Accommodation, banks with ATMs, post office, shops, bars, restaurants, buses and taxis. Tourist information office, tel. 922-555999. A Sunday market is held under a huge eucalyptus tree.

There is a steep climb at the end, onto an ash cone to finish in El Frontera

Extension to Charco Azul

Walk downhill as signposted for Charco Azul, on a very rocky, stony, narrow path flanked by walls. Turn left along a road, then right down a track. There are only two houses, so turn left before the second, along an easy path to a car park. The path gives way to fenced zigzags and steps, down to a rock pool and arch at **Charco Azul**. Retrace steps afterwards. The distance there and back is 3km (2 miles), with a descent and re-ascent of 100m (330ft).

WALK 41

El Frontera and Los Llanillos

Distance	8 or 9km (5 or 5½ miles)
Start	Tigaday, El Frontera
Finish	Los Llanillos
Alternative Finish	Las Casas, El Pinar
Total Ascent	500 or 1080m (1640 or 3545ft)
Total Descent	550m (1805ft)
Time	3 or 4hrs
Terrain	Roads, tracks and paths climb steep, forested slopes. The main descent can be overgrown, while the alternative descent is clearer.
Refreshment	Bars at El Frontera and Los Llanillos. Bar at Las Casas.
Transport	Buses link El Frontera and Los Llanillos. Buses serve El Pinar from La Restinga, San Andrés and Valverde.

This route uses steep roads and old tracks to climb from El Frontera towards the crest of El Hierro, then down to Los Llanillos. Landscapes vary from cultivated slopes to laurisilva and pine forest. There is an option to descend the far side of the island to El Pinar.

Route uses PR EH 2 and PR EH 2.1.

The start of this walk is difficult to find on the main street in **Tigaday, El Frontera**. Across the road from the Supermercado Yanira is the Novedades Conda. A road climbs from it but has no name-plate. (Ask a local person to confirm it as the Camino de San Salvador.) The road climbs and steepens, changing from tarmac to concrete, passing a couple of wine presses. Turn left along a path after the last house. This path, still the Camino de San Salvador, later drops to a road bend. Turn right, then left up a crunchy pumice path, winding up a slope of vines. Cross the main road to continue up the path, entering the Parque Rural Frontera.

Wind further uphill, passing scrubby terraces and heather trees. Watch for a wine press before joining a narrow road. Turn right up the road, left along a level road, then right up a pumice path in a deep groove on a slope of heather trees. Reach a clearing where a small crater is planted with chestnuts. Climb a soft and crunchy path, cross a level track, and follow a worn groove up through heather trees to cross another track.

Climb past a small cultivated patch then follow a winding path up a slope of dense laurisilva. Cross a track in a clearing and keep climbing. The path winds up through the forest, reaching a clear area on a slope of black ash, with a view to the distant village of Sabinosa. When a signpost is reached, there is a choice of routes.

Map continues on page 205

There is a view of El Frontera and El Golfo when the forest parts on the descent

Turn right to follow the PR EH 2.2 down to Los Llanillos. (See below for an extension to visit El Pinar.)

The path winds down a well-wooded slope, less trodden than the one used for the ascent. The surface is grassy or covered in leaf mould, with few markers, but the route is obvious. Wind downhill until a track is reached and turn left to follow it to a house. Follow a bendy road down past farm buildings. Turn right down the main road then left through a gap in the roadside barrier. Follow a rugged path downhill, still with heather trees dotted around, while some parts are overgrown. A gentler, easier descent passes hen huts and a steep track drops to a road.

A signpost across the road points down a stony, stone-paved or rocky path, past a few heather trees into luxuriant bushy scrub. Reach a road and turn right down it, picking up a path winding steep and stony downhill, sometimes on lava flows. Pass a stout juniper and note how the path and its flanking walls broaden on the way down. Aloes grow among dense tabaibal.

Cross a road and drop quickly to another road. Cross this and go down again to land on the main road in **Los Llanillos**, where there is a signpost and map-board. To finish here, buses and bars lie to the left down the road. However, walking further downhill links with Walk 40 for El Frontera.

Extension to El Pinar

Turn left as signposted for the PR EH 2 and wind up the well-wooded slope. The path becomes broad, reaching the main road beside signposts for the Camino de San Salvador. Cross the road and climb among trees, up a track to pass through a walled enclosure containing an *ermita*. The path climbs from forest onto bare slopes of ash, levelling out among heather and passing a pine. Continue as marked to reach a road on the crest of El Hierro, around 1350m 4430ft. ◄

The road is part of the Camino de La Virgen; see Walk 44.

Cross the road to continue along the PR EH 2, or Camino de El Pinar. Pick up and follow a track straight downhill. At first it is flanked by laurisilva; then, after

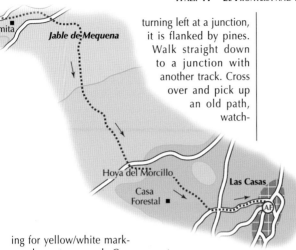

turning left at a junction, it is flanked by pines. Walk straight down to a junction with another track. Cross over and pick up an old path, watch-

ing for yellow/white markers down to a road. Cross over to reach a signpost near **Hoya del Morcillo**, around 100m (3280ft). Recreation area with an information hut, campsite, toilets, football pitch, play area and a huge El Hierro map made of wood and stones.

It is possible to walk straight ahead for El Pinar using the PR EH 1, reversing the start of Walk 38. However, there is another way to the village, by turning left to use the PR EH 3.1. A gravel track is followed a short way, then a vague track continues downhill with only a few markers, reaching a road. Turn right down it, then left to follow a track across a rocky streambed. Pines thin out, giving way to cultivated slopes with houses. Follow the track down to a road.

Turn left along the road, quickly reaching a crossroads on a main road. A signpost points down the quiet Calle El Calvario, reaching a junction at **Las Casas**. Turn right to reach the main road at a bend near the Bar Restaurant La Sabina. The rest of **El Pinar** straggles down the road towards Taibique.

WALK 42
Guinea and San Andrés

Distance	20km (12½ miles)
Start/Finish	Ecomuseo de Guinea
Total Ascent/Descent	1300m (4265ft)
Time	7hrs
Terrain	A steep and rugged ascent (if open), then easy tracks and paths, with a steep descent.
Refreshment	Bars at San Andrés and El Frontera.
Transport	Buses serve Guinea from El Frontera and Valverde. Buses serve San Andrés from Valverde, El Pinar and La Restinga.

This splendid circuit might not be fully open. A rock-fall occurred near the Ermita de La Peña and part of the path was closed. Check whether it is open or re-structure the route to start at La Peña, then head for San Andrés and finish at the Ecomuseo de Guinea (see Walk 43).

Route uses PR EH 8.

A map-board stands outside the **Ecomuseo de Guinea**, and a dusty track avoids using the main road in the direction of Las Puntas. When a junction is reached, sign-posted for La Hoya and La Ballena, follow a quiet road parallel to the main road, past scrubby fields and houses. Follow the main road past a water treatment building at **Pozo de Los Padrones**. Pass a road junction then look right for a walled, stone-paved track climbing to La Peña – if open.

The track narrows as it climbs, then it becomes stony as it crosses a slope of calcosas, verode, tabaibal and lavender. Enter the Reserva Natural Especial Tibataje. Parts of the path are strewn with stones and boulders, but the main ascent uses well-engineered stone-paved zigzags. Pass a sign at La Vuelta Grande overlooking **Las Puntas**.

Zigzag uphill and start a gentler traverse across steep slopes and cliffs, later overlooking a tunnel.

Cross gullies full of rock-fall debris and zigzag further uphill. Pass a small shrine and a sign for Calzada Ronpeculos. *Laursilva* begins to develop further uphill. The path levels out and more rock-fall debris is passed. The final zigzags are in excellent condition, reaching a narrow road above the unseen **Ermita de La Peña**. Turn right as signposted for San Andrés, continuing along a broad dirt road. ▶ The continuation of the walk from San Andrés is signposted as the PR EH 8 for Jinama and El Golfo, following a dirt road gently uphill away from the village. Turn left at a junction, then right, as signposted for the PR EH 8, and note also the presence of the GR 131. ▶ Follow the winding, gentle track right and left as marked, near a small area of tagasaste. Stay on the marked track, which eventually climbs to a road. Walk up the road and keep straight ahead, reaching a mapboard at the **Mirador de Jinama** and the Ermita Virgen de la Caridad. ▶

See Walk 32 for the route description as far as a junction on the outskirts of San Andrés.

See Walk 45 for more about the GR 131.

Enjoy fine views over El Golfo.

Easy signposted and waymarked tracks are followed near San Andrés

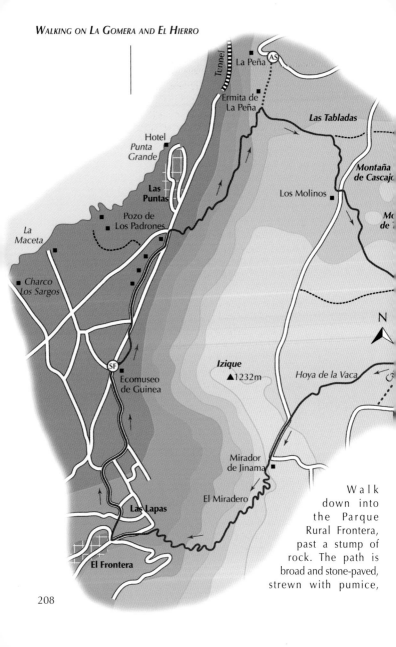

Walk down into the Parque Rural Frontera, past a stump of rock. The path is broad and stone-paved, strewn with pumice, zigzagging with fencing alongside. Pass a green gully and go down through laurisilva, past the Descansadero de la Virgen. Later, there is a view from **El Miradero**. Steep, boulder-paved zigzags run downhill. Turn round a hollow then climb a little to pass a rocky gap. Head down again, past Mocan de la Sombra and later pass a couple of big til trees on the way to Mocan de los Cochinos. A gentler path crosses a hump at Barranco las Esquinas. Zigzag further down and laurisilva gives way to scrub, while the last big tree is a pine.

Cross a road and leave the Parque Rural Frontera, later walking down the road a bit, then down a path on a slope of vines. A concrete road flanked by vines leads further downhill. Reach bend on the main road at El Frontera. Accommodation, banks with ATMs, post office, shops, bars, restaurants, buses and taxis. Tourist information office, tel. 922-555999. A Sunday market is held under a huge eucalyptus tree. Watch for a map-board and go straight down a steep, stone-paved track flanked by vines. A steep tarmac road, Calle Las Lapas, runs down through a crossroads, passing houses at **Las Lapas**.

Further downhill, pass a little plaza at Calle La Cruz and turn left down a steep, stone-paved road, reaching a tarmac road junction. Turn right down to a crossroads, walking straight ahead downhill for Guinea. Turn right at the bottom, along a level road. Avoid a road marked '*sin salida*' and continue past an unfinished building to reach a junction. Turn left downhill, passing lots of cultivated plots, while cliffs tower overhead. Follow the road down to the main road and turn right. Walk with care beside the main road to end back at the **Ecomuseo de Guinea**.

WALK 43
Las Puntas and Guinea

Distance	10km (6¼ miles)
Start/Finish	Punta Grande, Las Puntas
Total Ascent/Descent	100m (330ft)
Time	3hrs
Terrain	Mostly easy roads and paths, though some linking paths are rough and rocky.
Refreshment	Bars at Las Puntas, La Maceta and Los Sargos.
Transport	Buses serve Las Puntas and Ecomuseo de Guinea from El Frontera and Valverde.

This easy circuit is mainly along low-lying roads and tracks, hemmed in by the sea and steep cliffs at Las Puntas and Guinea. Some linking paths are rugged, crossing broken lava flows. Interesting features include the world's smallest hotel and the Ecomuseo de Guinea.

Route uses PR EH 8 and PR EH 8.1.

Start at a bus shelter at **Punta Grande**, near a tiny hotel on a rocky point. First, enjoy a short walk north along a broad, easy coastal path. This passes interesting little rocky points and inlets and is popular with fishermen. Go as far as a little building, enjoy views of the Roques de Salmor, and retrace steps to the road and bus shelter.

Walk along the road past the Restaurante La Mareta, rising gently past Cascadas del Mar. Hands are needed to climb onto rugged little cliffs. The ground is rough underfoot and the idea is to keep seaward of crude stone walls, passing headlands, coves and rock arches. Continue along a narrow walled path, rugged underfoot and overgrown, drifting away from the cliffs. Follow a seaward wall as flashed yellow/white then continue straight ahead along an easy track. ◀

Lots of aromatic incienso grows alongside.

Reputedly the world's smallest hotel on a rocky point at Punta Grande

The track heads gently down between a couple of properties, then when it heads inland, leave it to follow another path through a savage, black lava landscape. Some parts of the path are easy, with views of sea stacks. A car park and café are reached at **La Maceta**, where there are interesting rock pools.

It is worth following a spur route here, left of the Bar Restaurante La Maceta, up a stony track. Broken rock has been pushed aside and calcosas grows alongside. Pass a house to reach a road-end car park at **Charco Los Sargos**, beside the Kiosko Los Sargos. Again, there is

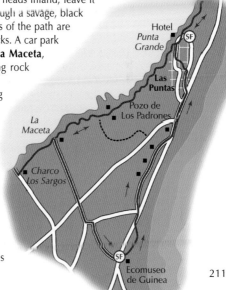

211

access to interesting rock pools. After exploring, retrace steps back to the car park at **La Maceta**.

Follow a road straight inland, past banana tents and a monstrous drystone wall. Go through a crossroads and pass a line of palm trees, then turn left past an old building, and right to reach the main road. Turn left and follow the main road to the **Ecomuseo de Guinea**.

The **Ecomuseo de Guinea** includes traditional farm buildings, representing life on El Hierro from the Conquest. The 'Lagartario' is where the native giant lizards of El Hierro (*Lagarto gigante*) are being conserved after almost becoming extinct. Check entry times in advance, tel. 922-555056.

A map-board stands outside the museum and a dusty track avoids using the main road in the direction of Las Puntas. When a junction is reached, signposted for La Hoya and La Ballena, follow a quiet road parallel to the main road, past scrubby fields and houses. Follow the main road past a water treatment building at **Pozo de Los Padrones**. Pass a road junction, then there is a signpost ahead for Las Puntas. Pass the Taqueria El Potrillo and a bus shelter, keep right, then later left, then keep left to follow the road to **Las Puntas**.

Pass a hotel and turn left after it to follow a short path. Cross a road then turn right down the stony Calle Punta Grande. Walk down to a tarmac road and retrace earlier steps past Cascadas del Mar to return to the bus shelter at **Punta Grande**.

WALK 44

GR 131: Orchilla to Fuente de Llanía

Distance	20km (12½ miles)
Start	Embarcadero, Orchilla
Finish	Fuente de Llanía
Total Ascent	1600m (5250ft)
Total Descent	100m (330ft)
Time	7hrs
Terrain	Mostly good tracks and paths. Bare ash slopes at the start become well vegetated and forested later. More bare ash on the mountains.
Refreshment	None
Transport	None

Every four years, on the first Saturday in July (count from 2013), a statue of the Virgin is carried from the Ermita de los Reyes to Valverde, accompanied by thousands of pilgrims. The Camino de la Virgen forms the central part of the coast-to-coast GR 131 over the mountains of El Hierro.

Start early at the western end of El Hierro, arriving by taxi or by arranging a lift along dirt roads to Orchilla. Leave the **Embarcadero**, a bleak picnic site among twisted lava beside a concrete pier. The GR 131 runs back up the dirt road and keeps right at a junction to avoid a lighthouse, **Faro de Orchilla**. The road runs round the ash slopes of **Montaña de Orchilla** and there is later a spur path down to the left, the GR 131a, offering an alternative start from the **Monumento al Antiguo Meridiano Cero**. ▶ Anyone visiting the monument must walk there and back as there is no access for vehicles.

The dirt road runs level round a bend, crossing a small bridge. Turn right as flashed red/white up a stony slope of tabaibal and incienso. A path short-cuts a road

Route uses GR 131.

Marks the original 'zero meridian', at the edge of the known world until Columbus voyaged further in 1492.

bend then a longer path climbs further. Cross the road again and look a little left to spot the continuation uphill. The path is

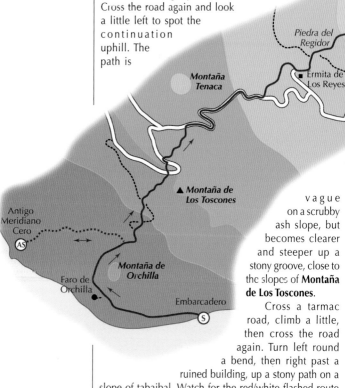

vague on a scrubby ash slope, but becomes clearer and steeper up a stony groove, close to the slopes of **Montaña de Los Toscones**.

Cross a tarmac road, climb a little, then cross the road again. Turn left round a bend, then right past a ruined building, up a stony path on a slope of tabaibal. Watch for the red/white-flashed route veering left on a stony slope. Reach a road and turn right, climbing round bends and later crossing a cattle grid. Turn left along a track past tabaibal and thyme, then branch right along a narrow path to climb to a gate. Climb higher, passing cave houses to reach Cueva de la Virgen. Turn right before the cave to the **Ermita de los Reyes**.

Look inside the **Ermita de los Reyes** to see the doll-like statue of the Virgin, which is carried on the day of the 'Bajada'. The statue resided at Cueva de la Virgen from

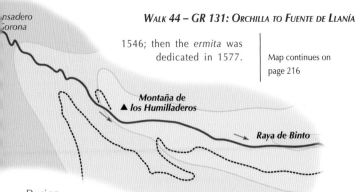

1546; then the *ermita* was dedicated in 1577.

Map continues on page 216

During a severe drought in 1614, shepherds carried the statue to Valverde and, miraculously, it poured with rain. The route to Valverde, the Camino de la Virgen, has been precisely measured as 28,686 metres (17¾ miles). On the day of the *Bajada*, pilgrims assemble at 5am.

Leave the *ermita* and walk up the road alongside, then along a dirt road to reach a complex junction at **Piedra del Regidor**. A map-board and signposts indicate

Good tracks follow, or run very close to, the mountain crest of El Hierro

several destinations, but simply climb straight ahead as marked and signposted for the GR 131 and Camino de la Virgen. Watch for distance posts beside the track, the first stating that 835m (½ mile) has been covered.

Prickly pears and junipers grow beside the walled track. Keep climbing past junctions with other tracks, then swing left further uphill. When a fork is reached, head right and the track is fenced on either side. Walk straight past a junction and a distance post for 2000m (1¼ miles). Climb to a GR 131 sign and turn right to pass **Descansadero La Gorona**, at 980m (3215ft). Keep right to climb further, peeping over a cliff edge for views.

The Camino de la Virgen is roughly aligned to a high crest. Keep left at junctions with other tracks, rising past a house and fields. The track pulls away from the crest but still climbs, winding past fields and patches of tree heather. Go through gates and cut across the steep ash slopes of **Montaña de los Humilladeros**. ◄ Pass a distance post for 4000m (2½ miles). Turn right to follow a broad track, past Cruz de los Humilladeros. The altitude is 1220m (4000ft) and there are views back to the *ermita* and Orchilla.

Further along, pass a Camino de la Virgen sign and go up a less obvious track on the left. Trees have been planted to regenerate the laurisilva. The track becomes grassy and slices across another track. Later, the track is rough and stony and the slope is covered in clumps of heather. Cross a bare ash slope, then rise through pine forest on a good track. Leaving the trees, a distance post for 6000m (3¾ miles) is passed. Cross another slope of ash and scrub, then curve and climb to reach Fuente de Binto at 1380m (4525ft).

Climb steeply up the ash slope, levelling out at **Raya de Binto**. The high-level track has

There are trees, but large areas are bare.

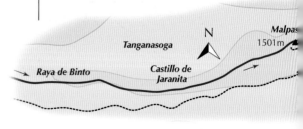

The route runs easily across the summit of Malpaso, the highest point on El Hierro

retaining walls then an ash path crosses a slope, followed by a dip and a gentle ascent to the 8000m (5 miles) marker. Pines, heather trees and scrub are passed as the path climbs in a little rocky valley, passing a signpost at Castillo de Jaranita. ▶

Walk 38 heads left for Sabinosa.

After climbing, go down through a rocky cutting, leave the sparse pines and climb up another ash slope. Keep left at a signpost and the path is marked by parallel lines of stones. Cross a dirt road on top of **Malpaso**, where there is a tall mast

Mirador de La Llanía

F

Fuente de
La Llanía

Jable de Mequena

1387m ▲ *Tábano*

Cruz de
Los Reyes

This is the highest point on El Hierro and views encompass the whole island. The islands of La Palma, La Gomera and Tenerife are often in view.

and a trig point at 1501m (4925ft). ◄ A monument commemorates the island-hopping GR 131 and its incorporation into the pan-European E7 route.

Follow the dirt road across a dip beyond the summit and pass a twisted juniper trunk and a distance post for 10,000m (6¼ miles). Climb a little, then keep left of the dirt road to follow a path. This runs down and clips a bend on the road. Keep left again and pass heather trees and pines, walking down an ash slope to reach a broad dirt road. Follow this as signposted, up through a cutting to reach a tarmac road and wooden cross at **Cruz de Los Reyes**.

Keep right of the cross, through a little avenue of pines, later turning right and left through a patch of laurisilva. Steer a course between a line of telegraph poles and the crest of the ridge, following a line of stones marking the route. The stones lead almost to the summit of **Tábano** at 1387m (4550ft). Walk down below a cliff to reach Raya del Cepon and a distance post for 12,000m (7½ miles). Walk up another ash slope, and follow a line between pines and the crest. The path becomes broad and clear, crossing steep, loose ash slopes. The path enters laurisilva and swings right to reach the road.

Turn left to follow the road onwards, or feel free to walk on bare ash beside it. Pass stumps of rock at Dos Hermanas, then note the PR EH 2 crossing the road. (The extension of Walk 41 goes this way to El Pinar.) A little further along the road, a sign indicates the Camino de la Virgen drifting left into forest. It becomes overgrown and it is better to stay near the road. The road quickly reaches a junction at **Fuente de La Llanía**, at 1335m (4380ft). Water taps are located near a roadside parking space in dense laurisilva, and this is a handy place to be collected. If there is time to spare, it is worth a short climb, as signposted, to the **Mirador de La Llanía**, for a fine view over El Golfo.

WALK 45

GR 131: Fuente de La Llanía to Estaca/Tamaduste

Distance	17.5km (11 miles)
Start	Fuente de La Llanía
Finish	Puerto de La Estaca
Alternative Finish	El Tamaduste
Total Ascent	150m (490ft)
Total Descent	1510m (4955ft)
Time	6hrs
Terrain	Mostly good tracks and paths, with some roads. Gradients are mostly gentle but steep towards the end.
Refreshment	Bars at San Andrés, Valverde, Puerto de La Estaca and Tamaduste.
Transport	Buses link San Andrés with Valverde, and Valverde with Puerto de la Estaca and Tamaduste.

The GR 131 runs mostly downhill from Fuente de La Llanía to San Andrés, Tiñor and Valverde. The route splits to leave Valverde, one spur heading to Puerto de La Estaca for the ferry, the other heading to El Tamaduste near the airport. Both descents are steep and rugged.

Start at Fuente de La Llanía and follow the main road for Valverde through tall laurisilva. Walk gently down the road, past a turning for Hoya del Morcillo, across a slight dip, rising gently to a sign reading 'Fileba' at 1300m (4265ft). There is a Camino de la Virgen sign on the left and the path roughly follows telegraph poles across an ash slope. ▶ The path passes a distance post for 16,000m (10 miles) on the way into a pine forest and towards the main road.

Follow the road through the forest, leave the trees and climb gently uphill at **Raya La Mareta**. Watch for a Camino de la Virgen sign on the right and follow a broad

Route uses GR 131.

It is worth climbing to a mirador overlooking a crater at **Hoya de Fileba.**

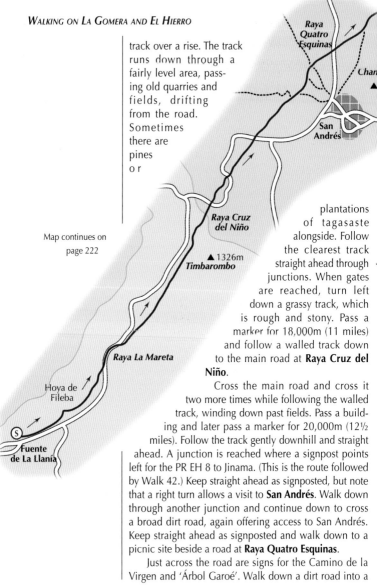

track over a rise. The track runs down through a fairly level area, passing old quarries and fields, drifting from the road. Sometimes there are pines
o r

Map continues on page 222

plantations of tagasaste alongside. Follow the clearest track straight ahead through junctions. When gates are reached, turn left down a grassy track, which is rough and stony. Pass a marker for 18,000m (11 miles) and follow a walled track down to the main road at **Raya Cruz del Niño**.

Cross the main road and cross it two more times while following the walled track, winding down past fields. Pass a building and later pass a marker for 20,000m (12½ miles). Follow the track gently downhill and straight ahead. A junction is reached where a signpost points left for the PR EH 8 to Jinama. (This is the route followed by Walk 42.) Keep straight ahead as signposted, but note that a right turn allows a visit to **San Andrés**. Walk down through another junction and continue down to cross a broad dirt road, again offering access to San Andrés. Keep straight ahead as signposted and walk down to a picnic site beside a road at **Raya Quatro Esquinas**.

Just across the road are signs for the Camino de la Virgen and 'Árbol Garoé'. Walk down a dirt road into a

Several volcanic ash cones are passed near the village of San Andrés

forest, up past a junction and over a rise to pass a distance post for 22,000m (13½ miles). Enter the Paisaje Protegido Ventejís; when a fork is reached, where 'Árbol Garoé' is signposted up to the left (Walk 32 goes this way), keep right along the Camino de la Virgen. The track runs level beside fields. Turn right at a junction to climb at **Raya Tejeguete**. Once over a rise, turn left and right downhill as marked, to follow a grassy, boulder-paved track.

Walk down to the main road and cross it, continuing down a rugged track, Camino Subida Tiñor, which has water pipes and cistus alongside, while heather trees cover the slopes. Walk straight down past a white chapel in **Tiñor**, ▶ and continue as signposted down the Camino Central Tiñor. Apart from a vegetated track, the road is brick-paved. Continue along the Camino La Placita to reach a bus shelter beside the main road.

Avoid the main road and follow a rugged tack and path parallel. Cross the road later and follow an undulating path across a slope of aloes, with a water pipe alongside. Wind down to cross the road and climb the other side, then follow the path through a groove cut into pumice and ash. Look into a crater at **La Caldereta** then go through a cutting for a view of Valverde. Zigzag downhill and cross the main road, stepping over a barrier.

A steep stone-paved road leads downhill, later surfaced in tarmac as Calle Casañas Frias as it reaches houses. Turn right down a steep, winding, one-way street, Calle Fernandez Armas, which passes near a museum, Casa de las Quinteras Centro Ethnográfico. Go under an arch then branch right down Calle Licenciado Bueno in the centre of Valverde. Depending on the final destination, either turn right for the Pub La Casita, or left to reach the church. ◄

On the day of the Bajada pilgrims finish with Mass in the church at 10.30pm.

To Puerto de La Estaca

From opposite the Pub La Casita in **Valverde**, walk up the brick-paved Calle San Francisco, climbing steps at the top. Go behind a supermarket and pick up the main road as it leaves town. Turn left down a side road and watch for a GR 131 signpost to follow a walled path downhill. This turns left and right while prickly pears, aloes, tabaibal, verode and calcosas grow alongside. Avoid turnings marked as 'private'. Note the buildings across the barranco, which is a goat farm. The broad and rugged path is the Camino Ancho, or 'broad way'.

At a junction turn right for the GR 131, following a narrower path. The path is gently graded, flanked by walls and aloes, then descends in a series of pronounced loops to the main road. Turn right to walk down the bendy road, enjoying bird's-eye views of the port. Turn left down an access road to pass a house and barking dogs. Go down an ash path and log steps, swinging right and left down the stone-paved Calle García Escamez, to reach a map-board at the bottom in **Puerto de La Estaca**, where a bar is available.

Raya Tejeguete

Chamuscada
▲1136m

To El Tamaduste

Leave the church in **Valverde** down Calle Doctor Gost, past the Hotel Boomerang, reaching a road junction and map-board. Walk straight ahead and continue along the level Calle la Carrera to reach a main road. Cross over and follow a narrow, brick-paved road. Turn right, then quickly left, down a road alongside a large building.

Walk off the end of the road, down a stony groove, then down log steps on a slope of black ash, passing aloes and calcosas bushes. Walk

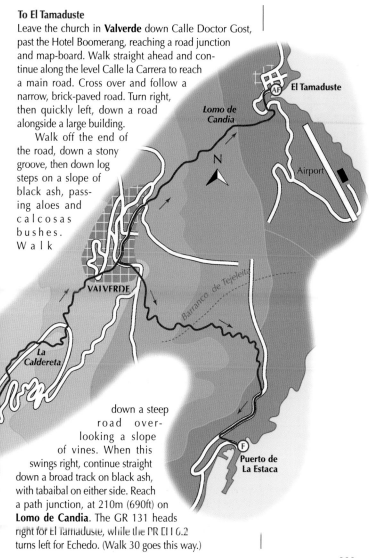

down a steep road overlooking a slope of vines. When this swings right, continue straight down a broad track on black ash, with tabaibal on either side. Reach a path junction, at 210m (690ft) on **Lomo de Candia**. The GR 131 heads right for El Tamaduste, while the PR EI 1 6.2 turns left for Echedo. (Walk 30 goes this way.)

One option for finishing the GR 131 leads down to a rocky cove at El Tamaduste

Turn right to walk down a rough cobbled path along the cliff edge. Swing left later and wind down past a rock outcrop. A concrete path drops in front of two houses and steps lead down to a road and pedestrian crossing. Cross and walk down more steps, short-cutting a road bend to reach **El Tamaduste** at the head of a cove. Explore around the cove and note that there are a couple of bars, a shop and buses. El Tamaduste is also close to the airport.

This is the end of the book, but not the end of the trail, as the GR 131 is an island-hopping route planned to stretch across all seven Canary Islands.

APPENDIX A

Route summary table

No	Start	Finish	Distance	Distance	Total Ascent	Total Descent
La Gomera						
1	Plaza de la Constitución, San Sebastián	Plaza de la Constitución, San Sebastián	18km (11 miles)	5hrs	700m (2295ft)	700m (2295ft)
2	Degollada de Peraza	Degollada de Peraza	8.5km (5¼ miles)	4hrs	700m (2295ft)	700m (2295ft)
3	Degollada de Peraza	Degollada de Peraza	15km (9½ miles)	6hrs	600m (1970ft)	600m (1970ft)
4	Roque de Agando	Playa de Santiago	13km (8 miles)	5hrs	75m (245ft)	1200m (3935ft)
5	Pajaritos, Alto de Garajonay	Playa de Santiago	15.5km (9½ miles)	4hrs	75m (245ft)	1450m (4760ft)
6	Chipude	Vueltas, Valle Gran Rey	10km (6¼ miles)	3hrs30	40m (130ft)	1100m (3610ft)
7	Chipude	El Guro, Valle Gran Rey	5/7.5km (3/4½ miles)	2hrs45/3hrs30	350m (1150ft)	350m (1150ft)
8	La Laguna Grande	La Laguna Grande	11km (7 miles)	4hrs	400m (1310ft)	400m (1310ft)
9	El Cercado	Valle Gran Rey	8km (5 miles)	5hrs	600m (1970ft)	600m (1970ft)
10	Las Hayas	La Calera, Valle Gran Rey	12km (7½ miles)	4hrs	190m (625ft)	1130m (3710ft)
11	Vallehermoso	Chorros de Epina	11km (7 miles)	4hrs	800m (2625ft)	180m (590ft)

225

No	Start	Finish	Distance	Distance	Total Ascent	Total Descent
12	Vallehermoso	Vallehermoso	13km (8 miles)	4hrs	740m (2425ft)	740m (2425ft)
13	Vallehermoso	Vallehermoso	14km (8¾ miles)	4hrs30	800m (2625ft)	800m (2625ft)
14	Vallehermoso	Vallehermoso	9km (5½ miles)	3hrs15	500m (1640ft)	500m (164Cft)
15	Simancas	Vallehermoso	7km (4½ miles)	2hrs	290m (950ft)	620m (2035ft)
16	Ibo Alfaro, Hermigua	Agulo	9km (5½ miles)	3hrs	800m (2625ft)	775m (2540ft)
17	Pajaritos, Alto de Garajonay	Museo Ethnográfico, Hermigua	13.5/20km (3½/12½ miles)	5hrs/6hrs30	150/350m (490/1150ft)	1350/1550m (4430/5085ft)
18	Santa Catalina, Hermigua	Santa Catalina, Hermigua	11km (7 miles)	4hrs	600m (1970ft)	600m (1970ft)
19	San Sebastián	Playa de Santiago	22km (13½ miles)	7hrs30	1050m (3445ft)	1050m (3445ft)
20	Playa de Santiago	La Dama	18km (11 miles)	6hrs	1320m (4330ft)	1100m (3610ft)
21	La Dama	Mirador del Santo, Arure	23km (14¼ miles)	8hrs	1570m (5150ft)	1090m (3575ft)
22	Mirador del Santo, Arure	Vallehermoso	15km (9½ miles)	6hrs	630m (2065ft)	1250m (4100ft)
23	Vallehermoso	Las Nuevitas, Hermigua	19km (12 miles)	7hrs	1000m (3280ft)	1100m (3610ft)
24	Las Nuevitas, Hermigua	San Sebastián	19km (12 miles)	6hrs	750m (2460ft)	850m (2790ft)
25	Igualero	La Dama	11km (7 miles)	5hrs	420m (1380ft)	1920m (6300ft)
26	Playa de Vallehermoso	Chipude	17.5km (11 miles)	7hrs	1500m (4920ft)	340m (1115ft)

No	Start	Finish	Distance	Distance	Total Ascent	Total Descent
27	Chipude	San Sebastián	25km (15½ miles)	8hrs	800m (2625ft)	1960m (6430ft)
	El Hierro					
28	Centre of Valverde	Centre of Valverde	9km (5½ miles)	4hrs	590m (1935ft)	590m (1935ft)
29	Centre of Valverde	Centre of Valverde	10km (6 miles)	5hrs	620m (2035ft)	620m (2035ft)
30	Centre of Valverde	El Mocanal	9.5km (6 miles)	4hrs	370m (1215ft)	420m (1380ft)
31	Centre of Valverde	Mirador de La Peña	10km (6 miles)	3hrs	270m (885ft)	200m (655ft)
32	Mirador de La Peña	El Mocanal	15km (9½ miles)	5hrs	480m (1575ft)	600m (1970ft)
33	Puerto de La Estaca	Puerto de La Estaca	14km (8¾ miles)	5hrs	1000m (3280ft)	1000m (3280ft)
34	Mirador de Isora	Mirador de Isora	15km (9½ miles)	6hrs30	1150m (3775ft)	1150m (3775ft)
35	Taibique, El Pinar	Cala de Tacorón	8km (5 miles)	3hrs	50m (165ft)	900m (2950ft)
36	Taibique, El Pinar	La Restinga	9km (5½ miles)	3hrs	50m (165ft)	900m (2950ft)
37	Ermita de Los Reyes	Taibique, El Pinar	17.5km (11 miles)	6hrs	550m (1805ft)	400m (1310ft)
38	Taibique, El Pinar	Sabinosa	16km (10 miles)	6hrs	670m (2100ft)	1190m (3905ft)
39	Ermita de Los Reyes	Ermita de Los Reyes	11km (7 miles)	3hrs	400m (1310ft)	400m (1310ft)
40	Sabinosa	El Frontera	12km (7½ miles)	3hrs15	200m (655ft)	150m (490ft)

No	Start	Finish	Distance	Distance	Total Ascent	Total Descent
41	El Frontera	Los Llanillos/ Las Casas, El Pinar	8/9km (5/5½ miles)	3/4hrs	500/1080m (1640/3545ft)	550m (1805ft)
42	Ecomuseo de Guinea	Ecomuseo de Guinea	20km (12½ miles)	7hrs	1300m (4265ft)	1300m (4265ft)
43	Punta Grande, Las Puntas	Punta Grande, Las Puntas	10km (6¼ miles)	3hrs	100m (330ft)	100m (330ft)
44	Embarcadero, Orchilla	Fuente de La Llanía	20km (12½ miles)	7hrs	1600m (5250ft)	100m (330ft)
45	Fuente de La Llanía	Puerto de La Estaca/ El Tamaduste	17.5km (11 miles)	6hrs	150m (490ft)	1510m (4955ft)

APPENDIX B
Topographical glossary

Apart from a few place-names derived from original Guanche words, most names appearing on maps are Spanish. Many words appear frequently and are usually descriptive of landforms or colours. The following list of common words helps to sort out what some of the places on maps or signposts mean.

Spanish	English
Agua	water
Alto/Alta	high
Arenas	sands
Arroyo	stream
Asomada	promontory
Bajo/Baja	low
Barranco	ravine
Barranquillo	small ravine
Blanco/Blanca	white
Boca	gap
Cabeza	head
Caldera	crater
Calle	street
Camino	path/track
Cañada	gully
Canal	watercourse
Carretera	road
Casa	house
Casa Forestal	forestry house
Caseta	small house/hut
Collada/Degollada	col/gap/saddle
Colorado/Colarada	red (blushing red)
Cruz	cross/crossroads
Cueva	cave
Cumbre	ridge/crest
De la/Del	of the
El/La/Los/Las	the
Embalse	reservoir
Era	threshing floor
Ermita	chapel/shrine
Estación de Guaguas	bus station
Fuente	fountain/spring
Gordo	fat/giant

Spanish	English
Grande	big
Guagua	bus
Hoya	valley
Ladera	slope
Llano	plain
Lomo	spur/ridge
Montaña	mountain
Morro	nose
Negro/Negra	black
Nieve	snow
Nuevo/Nueva	new
Paisaje	countryside
Parada	bus stop
Paso	pass
Pequeño/Pequeña	small
Pico	peak
Piedra	rock
Pino/Pinar	pine
Playa	beach
Plaza	town square
Presa	small reservoir
Puerto	port
Punta	point
Risco	cliff
Rojo/Roja	red
Roque	rock
San/Santa	saint (male/female)
Sendero	route/path
Valle	valley
Verde	green
Viejo/Vieja	old
Volcán	volcano

A cliff path cuts reasonably easily across the steep and rocky face of Risco de La Fortaleza (Walk 3)

APPENDIX C
Useful contacts

TRAVEL AND TRANSPORT
Inter-island flights
Binter Canarias, tel. 902-391392, www.bintercanarias.com

Inter-island ferries
Lineas Fred Olsen, tel. 902-100107, www.fredolsen.es
Naviera Armas, tel. 902-456500, www.naviera-armas.com

Bus services
Tenerife – TITSA, tel. 922-531300, www.titsa.com
La Gomera – Servicio Regular Gomera, tel. 922-141101
El Hierro – Transportes de Viajeros de El Hierro (TransHierro), tel. 922-551175

CANARY ISLANDS TOURISM
General tourism
www.turismodecanarias.com

Eco-tourism
www.ecoturismocanarias.com

Tourist information offices
La Gomera
San Sebastián, tel. 922-141512.
Playa de Santiago, tel. 922-895650
Valle Gran Rey, tel. 922-805458

El Hierro
Valverde, tel. 922-550302
El Frontera, tel. 922-555999
La Restinga, tel. 922-557114

ISLAND GOVERNMENT (CABILDOS)
La Gomera – www.cabildogomera.org
El Hierro – www.elhierro.es

FREE TRAIL MAPS
La Gomera – www.gomera-island.com/turismo/planos/mapasenderos.pdf
El Hierro – www.elhierro.es/files/images/mapa_senderos.pdf

Almond blossom appears early in the year, with the nuts themselves being gathered late in the year

NOTES

NOTES

NOTES

LISTING OF CICERONE GUIDES

Walking in the Harz Mountains
Walking in the Salzkammergut
Walking the River Rhine Trail

HIMALAYA

Annapurna: A Trekker's Guide
Bhutan
Everest: A Trekker's Guide
Garhwal and Kumaon: A
  Trekker's and Visitor's Guide
Kangchenjunga: A Trekker's
  Guide
Langtang with Gosainkund and
  Helambu: A Trekker's Guide
Manaslu: A Trekker's Guide
The Mount Kailash Trek

IRELAND

Irish Coastal Walks
The Irish Coast to Coast Walk
The Mountains of Ireland

ITALY

Central Apennines of Italy
Gran Paradiso
Italian Rock
Italy's Sibillini National Park
Shorter Walks in the Dolomites
Through the Italian Alps
Trekking In the Apennines
Treks in the Dolomites
Via Ferratas of the Italian
  Dolomites
  Vols 1 & 2
Walking in Sicily
Walking in the Central Italian
  Alps
Walking in the Dolomites
Walking in Tuscany
Walking on the Amalfi Coast

MEDITERRANEAN

Jordan – Walks, Treks, Caves,
  Climbs and Canyons
The Ala Dag
The High Mountains of Crete
The Mountains of Greece
Treks and Climbs in Wadi Rum,
  Jordan
Walking in Malta
Western Crete

NORTH AMERICA

British Columbia
The Grand Canyon

The John Muir Trail
The Pacific Crest Trail

SOUTH AMERICA

Aconcagua and the Southern
  Andes
Torres del Paine

SCANDINAVIA

Trekking in Greenland
Walking in Norway

SLOVENIA, CROATIA AND
MONTENEGRO

The Julian Alps of Slovenia
The Mountains of Montenegro
Trekking in Slovenia
Walking in Croatia

SPAIN AND PORTUGAL

Costa Blanca Walks
  1 West
  2 East
Mountain Walking in Southern
  Catalunya
The Mountains of Central Spain
Trekking through Mallorca
Via de la Plata
Walking in Madeira
Walking in Mallorca
Walking in the Algarve
Walking in the Canary Islands
  2 East
Walking in the Cordillera
  Cantabrica
Walking in the Sierra Nevada
Walking on La Gomera and
  El Hierro
Walking on La Palma
Walking the GR7 in Andalucia
Walks and Climbs in the Picos
  de Europa

SWITZERLAND

Alpine Pass Route
Central Switzerland
The Bernese Alps
Tour of the Jungfrau Region
Walking in the Valais
Walking in Ticino
Walks in the Engadine

TECHNIQUES

Indoor Climbing
Map and Compass

Mountain Weather
Moveable Feasts
Outdoor Photography
Rock Climbing
Snow and Ice Techniques
Sport Climbing
The Book of the Bivvy
The Hillwalker's Guide to
  Mountaineering
The Hillwalker's Manual

MINI GUIDES

Avalanche!
Navigating with a GPS
Navigation
Pocket First Aid and Wilderness
  Medicine
Snow

For full and up-to-date
information on our ever-
expanding list of guides,
visit our website:
www.cicerone.co.uk.

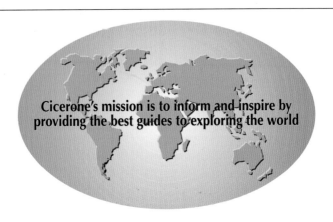

Cicerone's mission is to inform and inspire by providing the best guides to exploring the world

Since its foundation 40 years ago, Cicerone has specialised in publishing guidebooks and has built a reputation for quality and reliability. It now publishes nearly 300 guides to the major destinations for outdoor enthusiasts, including Europe, UK and the rest of the world.

Written by leading and committed specialists, Cicerone guides are recognised as the most authoritative. They are full of information, maps and illustrations so that the user can plan and complete a successful and safe trip or expedition – be it a long face climb, a walk over Lakeland fells, an alpine cycling tour, a Himalayan trek or a ramble in the countryside.

With a thorough introduction to assist planning, clear diagrams, maps and colour photographs to illustrate the terrain and route, and accurate and detailed text, Cicerone guides are designed for ease of use and access to the information.

If the facts on the ground change, or there is any aspect of a guide that you think we can improve, we are always delighted to hear from you.

Cicerone Press
2 Police Square Milnthorpe Cumbria LA7 7PY
Tel: 015395 62069 Fax: 015395 63417
info@cicerone.co.uk www.cicerone.co.uk

CICERONE